Love: Fall In Love Again

Marriage Advice for a Lasting Relationship

Rekindle Love and Take Back Your Marriage

5th Edition

By

Sofia Price

Sofia Price

© Copyright 2015 – 2020 – All rights reserved.

In no way is it legal to reproduce, duplicate, or transmit any part of this document in either electronic means or printed format. Recording of this publication is strictly prohibited, and any storage of this document is not allowed unless with written permission from the publisher. All rights reserved.

The information provided herein is stated to be truthful and consistent, in that any liability, in terms of inattention or otherwise, by any usage or abuse of any policies, processes, or directions contained within is the solitary and utter responsibility of the recipient reader. Under no circumstances will any legal responsibility or blame be held against the publisher for any reparation, damage, or monetary loss due to the information herein, either directly or indirectly.

Respective authors own all copyrights not held by the publisher.

Legal Notice:

This book is copyright protected. This is only for personal use. You cannot amend, distribute, sell, use, quote, or paraphrase any part of the content within this book without the consent of the author or copyright owner. Legal action will be pursued if this is breached.

Disclaimer Notice:

Please note the information contained within this document is for educational and entertainment purposes only. Every attempt has been made to provide accurate, up-to-date, and reliable, complete information. No warranties of any kind are expressed or implied. Readers acknowledge that the author is not engaging in the rendering of legal, financial, medical, or professional advice.

Table of Contents

Introduction 11

Chapter One: Pillars of Marriage 15

Pillar #1: Unconditional Love and Acceptance 16

Pillar #2: Faithfulness and Safety 18

Pillar #3: Mutual Respect 20

Pillar #4: Forgiveness 21

Chapter Two: Why Love Fades 23

Cheating 24

The Honeymoon Phase is Over 25

Window Shopping 26

Lack of Boundaries 27

Lack of Communication 27

Staying Away for too Long 28

Couples Tend to Let Go of Themselves Mentally and Physically 29

It Exhausts You to be With Him 29

Incompatibility 30

Taking Each Other for Granted 30

Not Telling Them You Love Them 30

Jealousy or Betrayal 31

Sex Has Become Routine 31

The Relationship Is Routine 32

The Ideal Future Does Not Include Your Partner 33

You Are Together for Other Reasons 33

Just Plain Bored 33

Chapter Three: Love Yourself 35
Acknowledge and Pursue Your Own Interest 36
Take Care of Your Looks and Your Health 40
Acknowledge Your Needs, Emotions, and Preferences 44
More Tips 47

Chapter Four: Nurture your Friendship 53
Importance of Friendship 53
Tips to Strengthen Your Friendship 58

Chapter Five: Take Your Commitment Seriously 69
Importance of Commitment 70
Levels of Commitment 71
Tips to Strengthen Commitment 73

Chapter Six: Secrets of a Successful Marriage 79
Retain Your Independence 79
Communicate in Each Other's Love Language 80
Learn to Listen 81
Accept Responsibility 81
Agree to Disagree 82
Don't Take Each Other for Granted 83
Intimacy Matters 84
Stay Romantic 85
Incorporate Date Nights 85
Search for Soft Emotions 86
Exchange Compliments 87
Accept the Reality 88

Never Mention the D Word.. 89
Stop Trying to Control... 89

Chapter Seven: Reminisce About the Happy Times 91
Savoring the Past... 92

Chapter Eight: The Appreciation Plan 97
Remember All the Good Things that Your Partner Has Done for You 98
Write Down All the Qualities that You Like about Your Partner 99
Read the List... 100
Share the List with Your Partner or Spouse 101
Silence the Critic Within You and Affirm Your Partner Often 102

Chapter Nine: Rekindle the Spark 105
It's a Date! 105
Check-In 106
Spend More Time Together 107
Be Affectionate toward Your Partner, Both Physically and Verbally 109
Share New and Exciting Experiences 111
Be Kind 113
Listen 114
Surprise Your Partner Often 116
Don't Go to Bed Angry 118
Remember Why You Fell in Love in the First Place 119
Profess Your Love Often and in Many Ways 120
Take a Break 122
Make Each Other a Priority 124

Chapter Ten: Improving Communication 127
Steps to Improve Communication 132

Chapter Eleven: Love Language 135
Types of Love Languages 135

Chapter Twelve: Healing Negative Cycles in a Relationship 145
Issue #1: The Blame Game 145
Issue #2: Emotional Distancing 148
Issue #3: Trust Fades Away 150
Issue #4: The Harsh Critic 152

Chapter Thirteen: Deal with Arguments 155
Take a Break 157
Understand Limits 157
Find Some Balance 158
Try Meditation 158
Learn to Apologize 159
Start Forgiving 160
Is It a Real Problem? 160

Chapter Fourteen: Offer Sympathy Not Solutions 163

Chapter Fifteen: HEAL Technique 171
Step One: Hear 172
Step Two: Empathize 173
Step Three: Act 175
Step Four: Love 176

Chapter Sixteen: Proactive Therapy 179
Benefits of Proactive Therapy 180

How Does Proactive Therapy Work? 183

Chapter Seventeen: Creating Emotional Safety and Security 189

Techniques to Build Emotional Safety and Security 191

Tips to Improve Emotional Intimacy 197

Chapter Eighteen: Rekindling Your Passion 205

Fostering Emotional Intimacy 205

Rekindling Sexual Chemistry... 206

Chapter Nineteen: The Passion Ignition Plan............211

Share a Fantasy with Your Partner 211

Change Up the Sex Schedule..212

Be Adventurous 213

Cuddle Every Morning 213

Get Fit 214

Kiss Your Partner Passionately for at least 10 Seconds Everyday 215

Chapter Twenty: Love Is a Verb 217

Chapter Twenty-One: Enhancing Sex 223

The Importance of Performing Physical Activities Together 223

Basic Positions..227

Conclusion 235

References...239

Sofia Price

Introduction

Many people who have been in a relationship or marriage for a very long time often complain that they are losing the "fire" and spark in their relationship. Many couples are often bored and claim that they no longer feel butterflies in their stomach. They no longer feel the passion and the joy they felt when their relationship was still new. They no longer feel the "chemistry."

On a scale of 1 to 10, how would you rate your marriage? Would you say it's a solid 10, a 5, or somewhere in between? Do you believe there is some scope for improving the relationship you share with your partner? Do you want to rediscover the flame you believe is missing in the relationship, or maybe you want to improve how you communicate as a couple? If your answer is yes to all these questions, you are in the right place. Falling in love is quite easy, but everything that follows is the difficult part.

Think of your marriage as a plant. What will happen if you don't water a plant regularly? What happens to the plant if it doesn't get sufficient sunlight or the nutrients it needs? The plant will slowly wither away and die. The same logic applies to your marriage, too. As with any other relationship in life, it takes time, effort, unconditional love, and lots of patience to maintain a strong bond. Rekindling love, recommitting yourself to the marriage, and strengthening the bond are the three important aspects of a successful relationship.

In this book, you will learn to fall in love all over again. Do you remember the initial love-filled days of your relationship – the fire you felt, the butterflies in your stomach, and the joy you experienced? Do you want to feel all these things again? If you follow the advice in this book, you can rediscover the spark in your marriage.

In this book, you will learn about why love often fades, how to fall in love with yourself, and how to fall in love with your partner all over again. From reminiscing about the happy times to creating an action plan to appreciate each other and improving your communication, there are many topics covered in this book. It is filled with simple, practical, and easy tips and techniques you can use to reignite your relationship's passion.

If you are one of the many confused people who feel that your love and affection for your partner are fading away, then this book is for you. This book contains proven techniques and strategies that will help you bring back the passion, excitement, and enthusiasm you once had in your relationship. Read on to reignite that spark and save your marriage and partnership before it's too late.

Love: Fall In Love Again

FREE E-BOOKS SENT WEEKLY

Join North Star Readers Book Club
And Get Exclusive Access To The Latest Kindle Books in Self-Improvement, Personal Health and Much More...

TO GET YOU STARTED HERE IS YOUR FREE E-BOOK:

www.northstarreaders.com/fearless-you

Sofia Price

Chapter One: Pillars of Marriage

Marriage is a lawfully recognized union between two consenting adults. It's the public declaration that two individuals have decided to spend their life with each other through happiness and sorrows, sickness and health, and the ups and downs of life. Marriage can be perceived in different ways by different individuals. Some think it to be the simplest way to remedy any loneliness they experience, while others think of it as the quickest means to achieve their happily ever after. Some think of marriage as a fully automated machine that can function effectively and efficiently without intervention or external help and effort. Marriage is not about remedying loneliness or fulfilling a societal obligation. It's a conscious decision to spend your life with another individual. After all, it is a promise of being there for each other for better or worse!

Marriage is not a remedy to loneliness, it isn't easy, and it certainly doesn't work without any supervision. Any individual who enters into a marriage, believing any of the things mentioned earlier, is up for a reality check. One of the most common reasons marriages end these days is because people wake up one fine day and realize their expectations are not the same as the reality of marriage. As with anything else in life, marriage takes a lot of effort and time. After all, the good things in life – the ones who truly matter – never come easy. The great news is that once you commit yourself to marriage and are willing to make an effort, it is one of the most satisfying and fulfilling relationships you will ever have.

Marriage requires effort, trust, teamwork, and a lot of other essential attributes for success in life. Marriage has certain demands that go beyond the ones required for organizational success. It is essential that you understand the basic pillars of marriage before you learn to rekindle the spark in your relationship. Think of a marriage as a house. Every house needs some pillars, or else, the roof collapses. Regardless of the different social or cultural ideas about marriage, successful marriages rely on simple principles that cannot be overlooked. In this section, let's look at the four pillars of marriage.

Pillar #1: Unconditional Love and Acceptance

What is the first thing that comes to your mind when you think of marriage? Perhaps love is the first thought. Yes, love and acceptance are vital for a marriage. However, these two things need to be unconditional.

Love is a passionate feeling that stems from within and makes you feel warm and cozy. Love makes you sexually and emotionally attracted to your partner and more enthusiastic about spending time with him or her. There is one caveat when it comes to love and acceptance in a relationship. Unless they are unconditional, they don't strengthen the bond you share. It is quite easy to love and accept something when it is in sync with what you want. The real test of a marriage is to love and accept someone unconditionally, despite his or her flaws, weaknesses, and quirks. When love is unconditional, it gives marriage the strength required to survive any difficulties, challenges, obstacles, and unpleasant fights you have.

As no two individuals are alike, a difference in opinion is bound to crop up. Sooner or later, there will be arguments, disagreements, and fights. If your marriage is built on a strong foundation of unconditional love and acceptance, it strengthens your relationship. True love makes you and your partner selfless towards one another. If you demonstrate your love for your partner only when he or she does something right and withhold it when something goes wrong, it will slowly eat away at the bond you share. If you or your partner soon believe that you will not be loved or accepted the way you are, it creates emotional and mental turmoil. Imagine how difficult it would be if you start believing you are not worthy of true love.

Love and acceptance are also important for intimacy. Intimacy doesn't appear out of thin air. If you and your partner are not your true selves, put up a facade, or are worried about showcasing your intimate desires, fears, and worries, distance creeps into the relationship. Intimacy isn't about sexual intimacy alone. It's also about emotional and mental intimacy. This increases when you are free to share all your dreams, hopes, fears, desires, and worries without any inhibitions. Once you bare your souls to each other without the fear of judgment, it strengthens the bond. True intimacy comes from knowing each other inside out. If you know you can fearlessly be who you are and you will still be loved and accepted despite all your flaws, it gives you the strength required to be more intimate. As with anything else in a marriage, this is a two-way street. As long as both the partners commit to the marriage, all these things are possible.

It isn't just about loving and accepting each other the way you are, but it's equally important to express it. Regardless of all the love you feel for your partner, if you fail to show it to him or her, then he or she will never understand. This is where love languages step into the picture. The phrase "love language" is pretty self-explanatory. It's the language in which one expresses one's love for others. There are different ways in which we show our love for others. Some are quite vocal about it, while others allow their actions to do the talking. Learning and understanding your love language and that of your partner is vital for a marriage. You will learn more about all this in the subsequent chapters.

Pillar #2: Faithfulness and Safety

No matter how much love you feel, if there is no trust, how can you live together? Faithfulness isn't restricted to sexual fidelity, but it is also about emotional and mental fidelity. Being faithful to your partner, emotionally, mentally, and physically, is a given in any relationship. Even if fidelity is absent in one of these areas, distance creeps in. It also opens doors for another person to step into the picture. Two is company and three is a crowd.

Many wrongly believe that fidelity is about being physically faithful to another person. No, this isn't what it's about. For instance, emotional and mental fidelity means sharing your secrets, desires, and hopes with your partner without any inhibitions. You cannot grow together or stay in a relationship if you cannot have this kind of openness. Trust is often the culmination of several small moments where one person turns to the other in their time of need. If your partner is there for you on such occasions, it increases the trust you share. In marriage, it's not the big gestures that matter, but it's all the little things that do. When you know someone will always be there for you no matter what happens, it gives you immense courage to explore yourself and the world without reservations. However, this trust should never be taken for granted. Because trust is like a mirror, and even a slight crack can quickly shatter it. Both partners need to be faithful to one another.

Once you and your partner start being there for each other, it increases mutual trust. It gives you the confidence that you can deal with any disagreements or fights in a relationship without worrying about ending the marriage. For instance, if you or your partner starts panicking at the slightest sign of trouble, it soon becomes a self-fulfilling prophecy. When you know the other person will be there for you, even in times of trouble and need, it certainly enriches the relationship you share. A simple ground rule, such as, "I am not going anywhere, and it is perfectly okay to be angry or upset," acts as the cement for binding trust or faith in the relationship.

Both partners in the marriage should feel safe and secure. Safety and security are not just about satisfying a basic physical need but also about emotional and mental needs. Unless you trust your partner fully, you cannot feel safe or secure in the relationship. You need to have mutual trust that neither will do anything to hurt the other. This sense of security also gives you both the freedom required to show vulnerabilities and weaknesses without any worries. It also encourages both partners to be their genuine selves without any facades. It also gives you a chance to share each other's hopes and dreams.

If you are insecure about yourself or the bond you share with your partner, everything becomes a difficulty. Insecurity often leads to other problems, such as suspicion, disbelief, lack of understanding, or even a dominating and controlling attitude. None of these things are healthy or desirable. For instance, if you are insecure about the relationship, you might feel jealous or possessive whenever your partner goes out to meet his or her friends. Likewise, you might feel uncomfortable sharing your dreams and hopes if you think your partner will ridicule them. The absence of a sense of security prevents partners from being their true selves. Over a period, it can lead to frustration and misunderstandings.

As mentioned previously, faithfulness is important for strengthening the emotional bond shared between partners. This, coupled with a sense of security in the relationship, enhances the bond you share. A simple act that can gradually erode this sense of safety in a relationship is nagging. You might not have realized it, but nagging indirectly conveys the message, "I don't believe you will do your part." Avoiding such behavior helps shape and strengthen the relationship. You will learn more about communicating your needs and wants without creating negative patterns in the subsequent chapters.

Pillar #3: Mutual Respect

A relationship cannot survive without mutual respect. How can you possibly live with or love someone you don't respect? Respect isn't about fear of authority or position. Instead, it's an inherent desire to be considerate towards someone else's views, opinions, and beliefs. Learning to respect your partner's opinions, boundaries, and wishes are important for a marriage's health. How will you feel if all your opinions are disregarded? What if your partner treats you like you are not his or her equal? How will you feel if your partner doesn't respect your boundaries? All this can quickly add up and make you feel devalued. Loving someone you don't respect is not a sign of a good relationship. In a healthy relationship, partners not only love and accept each other the way they are, but there is also mutual respect.

When you respect someone, your inclination to willingly listen to this person increases, and when the other person feels heard and understood, it prompts him or her to reciprocate the same. Marriage is an equal partnership. If you contribute 50% to the marriage, your partner would do the rest. Doing this becomes easier when you respect each other. It also becomes easier to support each other unconditionally with respect. The simplest form of respect is to listen to what your partner says without brushing him or her off.

Pillar #4: Forgiveness

It's quite likely you have come across the phrase "forgive and forget." This is one of the things that are easier said than done. To truly forgive and forget, you need to have a certain level of mental and emotional maturity and discipline. It is human nature to make mistakes, and unless you deal with the mistakes, learn your lessons, and move on, they will slowly but certainly erode the bond between partners. Implementing the idea of forgiving and forgetting is not easy, but this is one quality that comes in handy in almost all aspects of your life.

No marriage is free of any issues. These issues can be both small and big. At times, it's the small issues that result in big trouble and the small offenses that manifest into bigger ones. If two individuals are living together, disagreements are bound to crop up. As you live and grow together, mistakes are also bound to happen. Learning to deal with all this is an important aspect of a marriage.

Some can forgive easily while others take some time. Understanding and accepting these differences in each other's temperaments offer scope for growth. If you cannot forgive or forget an issue, moving away from it and concentrating on the future becomes difficult. The failure to forgive or forget prevents you from living in the present and traps you in the past. Living in the past is not only troublesome for the marriage, but it also harms your overall wellbeing. As long as the incident in question doesn't damage any of the other pillars of the marriage, it can be handled. If you truly believe the relationship you share is worth fighting for, never forget the importance of forgiveness.

You will learn more about different tips and suggestions you can use to strengthen each of these pillars in your marriage.

Chapter Two: Why Love Fades

If you are reading this book, chances are, you feel that you are losing the passion and strong affection you once had with your spouse or your partner. If you are reading this book, it is most likely that you want to save the relationship that was once exciting, passionate, and loving. You are not losing hope that you can still save and bring back the "spark" in the relationship. You still believe the relationship can be saved.

You may remember how the relationship felt when it was new. You extremely adored each other. You could talk and discuss just about anything. You would frequently go out together, and you would do many fun and enjoyable activities together.

You used to hold hands and do cheesy things. You used to call each other a lot or send loving messages. You said kind words and shared a few laughs every day. You gave each other romantic things, such as loving messages, flowers, gifts, poems, and even letters.

You were playful with each other. Your relationship was filled with care, respect, and attraction. The sex was amazing. You touched a lot and made love often, but now, you wonder, what happened? How did a relationship so great become so boring? How can a relationship that was once filled with genuine love and respect only exist because of mere tolerance?

Maybe it is because you already have kids, and the children have become the priority. Maybe the love has faded because of the simple reason that you are already tired of each other. Falling in love is splendid and glorious; however, making love last for a lifetime is really challenging.

Before we discuss the ways in which you could fall in love with your partner again, it is important to understand why your love is fading. Here are the common reasons why it happens:

Cheating

If you have been thinking about this for quite some time, and you are looking for answers, then there is a possibility that things are not going too well in your relationship. You must understand that feelings will change over time, and the feeling of love you have for someone does not necessarily have to last forever. The two of you must remain honest with each other during this time. It is a terrible feeling to have to tell someone that you are not sure how you feel at the moment. You may not want to do this, but when you push them away without giving them any explanation, they will feel terrible. You cannot expect them to take a hint, and one of the worst things to do is to cheat on them.

Cheating does not only have to be physical. It can also be emotional. When you start losing feelings for your partner and start developing feelings for another person, you need to talk to your partner before you act. If there is a change in your behavior, your partner may have already sensed it. In fact, your partner may be experiencing something similar. You will feel terrible when you have this conversation, but you have not done anything wrong. So, make sure you have this conversation with your partner before you cross the line.

The Honeymoon Phase is Over

Do you remember the time when you loved everything your partner did for you? This may seem like a very long time ago, but every couple has been there. When you love someone, you will love everything that they are doing for you. You will find whatever they do captivating and amazing. You will have gushed about everything they did with your friends. Even the smallest things your partner did was something you wanted to let the world know about. This person was definitely marriage-worthy. If you do not find the things your partner does cute, it is a sign that love is fading. This relationship may not be working out for you two.

When you first start dating, you will have higher tolerance levels because everything looks rosy. These rose-tinted spectacles are definitely a blessing during the initial days. Things will change after a while, and you will see that you are both cruising along, except for a few arguments that you may have. If you are irritated because of small issues that crop up between the two of you, it is probably time for you to re-evaluate your relationship.

Small issues and minor problems can irritate you now, and you may find it difficult to forgive misjudgments or mistakes. You may also stop feeling guilty for doing the wrong things. When you no longer feel compassionate toward your partner, it is evident that you feel differently now. Things will change in any relationship, and there will come a time when there is a plateau.

Window Shopping

Let us be honest. You will find someone more attractive than your partner, and this is bound to happen. This does not mean you do not love your partner. There is nothing wrong if you want to appreciate someone's looks, but if you think about how it will be when you are with them, then there is something wrong at home.

As mentioned earlier, it is a terrible idea to act on any attraction or feeling you have toward a person who is not your partner. This is a huge no-no. This is something that anybody will agree on. Having said that, most people sabotage their relationships when they kiss someone else or take things a little too far when they text someone on Instagram, WhatsApp, or Snapchat. It gets worse when you do this with strangers. If you constantly think about ending your relationship, you need to be conscious and make the right decision. You should either talk to your partner or shut these thoughts down. If you feel very strongly about getting out of the relationship, then your partner may feel very strongly about it, too. Make sure you speak with your partner before you act in any situation like this. The conversation is going to be painful, but it is better than having to confess about doing something wrong.

If your partner has picked up a shift in behavior, you need to explain to him or her why it is that you feel this way. You owe at least this much to your partner. You cannot leave him or her worrying about whether you will stay. This will only ruin his or her self-confidence. You will be the one to blame because you could never be honest. You should always think about how it would be if you were on the other side.

Lack of Boundaries

Most people who fall out of love often say, "I do not know myself anymore." Merged identity is often the reason why passion and love fade in a relationship. When you spend a lot of time with someone, you could sometimes feel you have lost your identity and individuality. When you first fell in love, you had healthy boundaries that both of you were careful not to cross. However, as time goes by and you make decisions like living together and having kids, these boundaries disappear. Add the responsibilities of having a job, bills, and taking care of your family, and it's easy to feel like the person you were has faded away. You do not have sufficient quality time apart to become truer to who you really are and what makes you happy as an individual.

Lack of Communication

Many people fall out of love because of a lack of healthy communication. Conflicts are often unresolved. These couples no longer affirm their love and appreciation toward their spouse. Couples who have been together for a long time often do not express their needs to their partners. These couples often refuse to discuss serious relationship problems. This is the reason why frustrations pile up. When the negativity adds up, resentment can cause a relationship to become strained and uncomfortable. Communication is a powerful component of a good relationship, and it is a fact that a lack of sufficient communication between partners can dissolve a relationship.

Staying Away for too Long

When you initially start dating, you will want to be with each other every minute of every day. You will do anything you can to spend time together, and the times when you are not together; you will continue to keep in touch through cute texts and Snapchat. You will never get enough of each other, and this feeling is wonderful. You will leave a few earrings at his place, and he may leave his t-shirt at your place. Now, you spend a lot of time at each other's places. Regardless of whether you live together or visit each other, you want to stay together at all times because you will miss each other when you are not together.

It is definitely healthy to spend some time away from each other, but if you choose to spend too much time away from each other, then your feelings can definitely change. If you do not miss your partner too much, then something has changed. If the connection between the two of you has changed, then so have your feelings.

You may not reply to messages quickly and will not be the first to send messages to your partner any longer. These changes may not seem like too much, but a change in intimacy levels and affection is a very big issue. When this happens, you need to ask yourself what it means for your relationship.

Couples Tend to Let Go of Themselves Mentally and Physically

There will be a time when you reach a specific level of comfort in your relationship. When this happens, you often forget to take care of yourself and your needs. You are no longer conscious of how you look. You may have quit exercising, or you formed unhealthy habits, such as drinking too much alcohol or watching too much television. You also tend to stop doing things that mentally stimulate you. You stopped reading or taking advanced classes. When this happens, the physical and mental attraction you once had when you were just starting the relationship will eventually fade.

It Exhausts You to be With Him

You must understand that relationships do take work. That said, if it becomes too exhausting for you to stay in the relationship, you need to call it off. If you two love each other, you will find it in your heart to work on the relationship. If everything you do feels forced, then there is nothing in your relationship that will give you a boost. You will always feel exhausted when you spend time together. You need to give yourself a break and admit that you have fallen out of love. When you do this, you can work on the relationship.

Incompatibility

When the relationship is still new, you tend to project some things to your partner. You tend to be on our best behavior. However, as you move deeper into the relationship and spend more time with your partner, you discover that you may not be compatible. You may discover that your values and priorities are not aligned; this is often the reason why love fades.

Taking Each Other for Granted

This is one of the most common reasons why relationships fade. Partners or spouses often take each other for granted. They no longer check on each other, and they no longer pay attention to each other's needs.

Not Telling Them You Love Them

You can never force words to come out of your mouth. When you do not feel the emotions strongly, you will say these words much less. You will always find yourself changing the subject or smiling less whenever your partner tells you he or she loves you. This is one of the most noticeable signs, especially to your partner. You need to pay attention to how you say these words to your partner. If it does not feel right to you, tell him or her that you are falling out of love, and see what can be done to improve the relationship.

Jealousy or Betrayal

This one is huge; jealousy is sometimes a simple sign that your partner loves you. However, chronic jealousy can be overwhelming and intoxicating. When there is betrayal or jealousy in the relationship, there is no trust, and trust is one of the most important ingredients in any successful relationship.

Sex Has Become Routine

When the relationship is still new, you make love often and touch each other more frequently. After years of being together, sex can become a routine or more of a chore. Gone are the days of hot, passionate sex that helps you channel your creative orgasmic energy as a powerful fuel for your health, vitality, energy, and creativity. You no longer explore and passionately touch each other's bodies. Although sex is not the most important component of a relationship, it is still one of the major keys.

Some people do not think sex is important. For others, sex is the foundation of the relationship. Regardless of how good the sex is, if the number of times you have sex has decreased, it is a sign that your feelings have changed. It could be because:

- You no longer find your partner attractive
- You think about someone else when you have sex with them, and this leads to guilt
- There is a sudden shift in your feelings

You need to face these changes and explain them to your partner as well.

If you used to be the one to initiate sex and you find yourself turning down sex when your partner approaches you, you need to step up and speak with him or her. If you leave things as they are, it is only going to get worse for you. Let us reverse the situation. If you are the one who makes an effort and you have had a very good sex life, how would you feel if there was a sudden change in the way your partner behaved? You start getting dressed for your partner, try different things, put yourself out there, or even try roleplaying. Your partner, however, turns down all your advances. You are only going to start panicking about what this means for the relationship. Your self-confidence will also plummet.

Feeling rejected and undesirable is one of the worst emotions, and it will affect every aspect of your life. These feelings will also drive a wedge between your partner and yourself. Let us now reverse the roles. If you are the one causing these emotions in your partner, how do you think he or she will feel? Not too good, right? You need to understand these emotions in the beginning, so you save your partner the pain. He or she will no longer have to believe that something is wrong with him or her. You will learn to work together when your feelings are out in the open.

The Relationship Is Routine

You get up, kiss good morning, get ready for work, come back home, cook together or alone, eat together, watch a show, and fall asleep. This happens every day. The relationship is just another routine. There is nothing that you look forward to. You will think you are comfortable, but the trouble is that the relationship is boring and dull. You do not love your partner too much at all. You cannot expect love only to be a routine, and if it does feel that way, then something has to change.

The Ideal Future Does Not Include Your Partner

When you first started dating, your partner was your future, and you were his or hers. Now, when you think about your future, he or she does not feature in it. Your partner does not even make a guest appearance. You will see that you are living your dreams, but he or she is not a part of those dreams. You would have found a place for your partner if you were in love. As there is no love, you have moved on from your partner already.

You Are Together for Other Reasons

You may stay together for reasons that have nothing to do with any emotions. For example, you may no longer have the current financial support, and that thought scares you, or you may have children together. You are only staying in the current situation until it changes. You are not staying with your partner because you love him or her.

Just Plain Bored

When you are with your partner for a very long time, you routinely choose security over passion and excitement. Everything becomes a routine, and everything is planned; your relationship lacks spontaneity and passion. Planning is good; in fact, if you want to stay together for a very long time, it is best to plan ahead. However, if everything in the relationship is planned and calculated, you will eventually become bored.

It is no secret that staying in love is much harder than falling in love. Love, as they often say, is a choice. So, if you think that your relationship can be saved and it is still worth saving, it is time to act now before it is too late. The good news is that you can still rekindle that good old fire and spark. You can still ignite that fading passion and fall in love again. After all, marriage or partnership, according to experts, means falling in love with the same person many times.

Your partner will feel bad when you tell him or her that you have fallen out of love, but he or she will feel worse when you tell him or her that you have not been in love for a long time. When you tell your partner this, he or she will feel like you lied. Your partner will soon begin to question your recent actions, which will tear the relationship apart. This will drive your partner crazy. Make sure that you talk to your partner about how you feel. Yes, this will be painful for the two of you, but you must address this issue.

When you talk about the relationship, it may make you realize that you do not want to be with your partner. It may also give you a reality check, and you will understand what it is that you are doing wrong. This is never going to be an easy conversation, but you need to have this conversation with your partner. It is for both of your sakes. It is never a good idea to stay in a relationship and waste each other's time. This is not fair to either of you. When you begin to question your feelings, and you share them with each other, you can come to a decision together. This is the least you can do for your partner.

Chapter Three: Love Yourself

Many renowned psychologists say that you cannot love another person unless you first love yourself. The reason is actually pretty simple; you cannot give what you do not have.

To rekindle the passion in your relationship, you have to show unconditional love for yourself. You have to care about yourself. You have to acknowledge your individual needs, wants, desires, and preferences.

As discussed earlier, one of the reasons why people say their relationship has faded is because they have lost their sense of self. When people are in a relationship for a very long time, they become so engaged in caring for their partners or taking good care of their kids that they tend to neglect their own interests and needs. In addition to this, people who are in long-term relationships often tend to neglect their own health.

When you are in a relationship for a long time, you tend to not care about how you look. You quit exercising or going to the salon. You may begin to gain weight or lose your attractiveness. If you did let yourself go, chances are, you are not the only one slowly falling out of love. There is a big possibility that your partner is slowly falling out of love with you, too.

Do not panic if what has been described applies to you. These are all things that can be fixed by making better choices for yourself. Here are the ways to love yourself more to awaken your ability to love your partner completely.

Acknowledge and Pursue Your Own Interest

When you are with your partner or spouse for a long time, you may forget your individual dreams and interests. As discussed earlier, you may already share an identity with your spouse. When this happens, you will become frustrated, and that frustration will fuel your contempt and loss of interest in your partner.

While it is important for you and your partner to have some similar interests and hobbies, it is even more important to have your own. There are so many benefits to having your individual interests and aspirations. Firstly, it keeps your daily life fresh and engaging. Whether you take a painting class or you are writing a novel, you are taking a break from the monotony of daily life and doing something that excites you. While it may seem that leaving your spouse by him or herself for a while might not be the best idea, having your own interests could be a great way to talk about new things. You could discuss what you are learning or how your hobby makes you feel, whether you are exercising or creating something with your hands. Your spouse or partner could learn something from what interests you, and who knows, maybe he or she will be inspired to pick up a new hobby of his or her own.

Another reason why having individual dreams and interests is crucial is that it can make you a more passionate person. Think about what you love to do or think of someone who eats, sleeps, and breathes something important to them. It could be volunteer work, competitive dancing, or discovering new recipes. You know they are passionate about it because the emotions they feel about it radiate off of them. Their happiness is contagious and inspiring.

Love: Fall In Love Again

Find something that makes you feel like this. Find an interest that makes you want to get up and do it every day. This will relay into other areas of your life, including your marriage. If you are enthusiastic about the things that interest you, it will be easier to be enthusiastic about your relationship. You'll want to feel happy and euphoric about as much of your life as possible. This sort of mindset is infectious, and if you are positive, it could cause your partner to want to reciprocate. This passion for your interests could also cause you to feel passionate in other ways that might have gone dormant. Having a hobby could bring the spice and the spark back to your marriage, so go for it!

Having a hobby can give you serious self-confidence, especially if it's something you are good at. While this doesn't mean that you should be an expert or the best at everything you do, you should embrace the things that make you feel proud of yourself. Maybe you are naturally gifted, or you feel contented with how hard you have worked in an activity. Your life wouldn't be the same if you didn't have these accomplishments. The same can be said for your relationship; surely, there are elements of your relationship that give you self-confidence. Are you a good listener? Do you take your partner's quirks in stride? Try to make a comparison between how you feel when you excel in your interests and how you feel when things are positive with your partner. If you find yourself having a hard time making that connection, don't worry. Having confidence in yourself can help you talk to your spouse or partner or even show your partner how wonderful and exciting you are. Your partner could become intrigued by what "makes you tick" and may want to see this version of you more often.

Dreams and aspirations are important because they give you goals to work towards. Maybe you would like to run a marathon someday, or maybe you want to change the life of underprivileged children by becoming a mentor for them.

Regardless of what interests you, goals are great. They motivate you, give you something to work towards, and make you accountable. You often accomplish your dreams or goals, or there may be a reason why they don't work out. Once again, you can apply this to your relationship. Make a goal to tell your significant other that you love him or her at least once a day. Promise yourself that you will take the time to make your partner smile and remember why you fell in love in the first place. These little goals can eventually become part of larger goals. Perhaps you'll want to make healthier life choices to improve the quality of both your lives. Maybe make an effort to take your partner out somewhere fun. Think of how wonderful you'll both feel as these goals are accomplished. It's okay if completing these objectives takes time; if you are trying your hardest, your partner will see your efforts. It's better to try and struggle at something than never attempt it all. This can be said about hobbies, so why not a relationship?

Having interests and hobbies can inspire those around you. If your spouse or partner is seeing that a new or favorite activity is having such a positive effect on you, it may make him or her stop and think. It's giving you a renewed vigor, and it's forming you into a better version of yourself. If you are showing a willingness to try new things in life and a relationship, maybe this can also encourage your partner to put in extra effort as well. A relationship is a two-way street, and if your partner sees you trying your hardest to make things work, he or she may be persuaded to do the same.

Having something that you aspire towards gives your life meaning. In the previous example of a competitive dancer, if she wants to be the best that she can possibly be, it requires practice, dedication, and discipline. If she is passionate about dancing and is willing to do what it takes to see her dreams fulfilled, it becomes a part of who she is. In knowing what that feels like, she can apply that sense of purpose to other areas of her life, and so can you. Think of the things that make you want to better yourself and which you think gives your life meaning. The same can be said about your relationship. It takes work, but the results of feeling more in love with your partner are worth it.

Absence makes the heart grow fonder. Maybe part of the reason that things are troublesome in the relationship is that you lack independence and individuality because you are spending large amounts of time together. While it's great to spend time with each other, if you are focused on doing your own thing every now and again, your partner may have a greater appreciation of the time that he or she does spend with you. You may also find new things to talk about, and it could encourage you to break away from the day-to-day routine. Spending time apart could also benefit you, in the sense that the interests that you share could become more meaningful because you aren't doing these hobbies and activities together as often.

Take time to think of activities you want to do on your own, such as training for a marathon or attending a yoga class. It's never too late to find something that excites you and makes you happy. When you do the things you love, you become whole as a person. When you feel whole, and when you feel you are retaining your individuality, it is easier for you to fall in love with your partner again. A sense of purpose, independence, and individuality is also sexy. When you have a strong sense of purpose, you will become more interesting to your partner. When you are doing what you love, you bring a certain positive vibe and energy into the relationship, and it will help reignite the dwindling heat and passion. Positivity is contagious and can cause your partner to want to rekindle the flame as well.

Take Care of Your Looks and Your Health

What commonly happens is that you see a couple out and about, and you know that's not the person they originally married or had a relationship with. It's not that they are seeing someone else. It is just that the person they were, back when their partner fell in love with them, has faded and has been replaced with someone new. In some instances, both people in the relationship have fallen victim to this, and the dynamic of the relationship has changed; it's become bland.

In some cases, you may have eased up on your appearance and lost focus on your health because you and your partner have grown comfortable around each other. Maybe it used to make you feel nervous for your significant other to see you in your pajamas or without makeup, but now that you've been together for a while, those instances no longer scare you. While that is good in some ways, it could cause your partner to feel a loss of attraction towards you or vice versa.

On the other hand, the lack of effort could be because of a variety of other reasons. Daily life can be exhausting, and now that you're in a committed relationship, keeping up appearances is not high on your list of priorities. Don't let this happen! Not only will taking care of yourself benefit your partner, but it's also even more important for you to feel healthy and happy with your appearance.

Having self-esteem will make you feel better about yourself. If you take the time to take care of your appearance, you will feel happier, and that positivity will overflow into other areas of your life. Do you remember how it feels to get compliments on new outfits or a stylish new hair cut? Imagine the feeling you would get if your spouse or significant other were the one who noticed. Self-esteem is the foundation for self-worth. If you are positive about your appearance, then you can also gain positivity in other aspects of your life, such as your relationship.

Taking care of your health is also important. Maybe you have gained some weight, and your clothes don't fit anymore. Maybe you haven't been feeling 100% because you are eating the wrong kind of food and aren't exercising. That frustration and negativity can affect other aspects of life. Maybe your partner used to tell you that you looked attractive early on in the relationship and had since stopped. It's like a snowball effect; soon, your negative feelings about yourself are being reflected onto your partner, and it's no wonder that the relationship isn't what it used to be. Don't panic; anyone can turn him or herself around and start a new healthy lifestyle. Just like having goals with your hobbies, it takes hard work and discipline, but it can be achieved. Overcoming these obstacles as a couple can also bring you closer together.

Exercise is so good for you! Not only can it help you lose weight, but it can make you stronger. Once you get into the habit of working out, it can become part of your daily routine. Working out can be fun, and it makes you happier. Endorphins tell your brain that you are feeling good and relieve stress, which might also make you want to binge-watch your favorite television show or order take out more than just on special occasions. If you are feeling better because you are leading a healthier lifestyle, you could become happier about other things. Exercising can be beneficial for your relationship because you'll feel confident, and your partner will notice how trim you are appearing and the positivity you are feeling.

Eating healthier will also make you feel better about your health and body image. In a world full of fast food and processed food, it's easy to fall into the trap of eating poorly. There are so many easy changes that you can make to begin transforming your eating habits. Just by simply cutting out soda or other junk food, you could lose a few pounds. You can eat clean, and there are books and websites packed with dieting advice. When you eat better, you feel better. Eating the proper food can give you the energy you need to get things done. So, even if you don't lose weight right away, just by feeling healthier, you will be happier. The effort you put into these changes can make your partner look at you in a new light, and your newfound energy will help your spouse or partner remember why he or she fell in love with you in the first place.

Sometimes, it is not just you who has let your health go. Maybe you and your partner have both stopped taking care of your appearance. Attempting to improve your quality of life can encourage your spouse or partner to be motivated to look after his or her appearance and health as well. Not only can it be possible for you to be attracted to each other again if you are losing weight and taking care of your appearance, but you will be able to see that you are both putting in the effort to better yourselves for the sake of your marriage or relationship.

Taking care of your health can be something that you and your partner can have in common. You can work together to stay accountable for eating healthy or exercising a certain number of times throughout the week. It can serve as a bonding experience as you can go for a walk or try a new gym together. As regards clean eating, you can plan out your meals or try new recipes together. Most importantly, if your partner is trying his or her hardest to work on his or her appearance and health, you should support and praise him or her. Being positive and kind will make your partner more apt to return the gesture and make your bond stronger than ever.

You can improve your appearance and health without spending a lot of money. You can buy a few staple pieces for your wardrobe that can be mixed and matched with items you might already own. You don't need to go to a fancy hair salon; just find a place where you can get an affordable haircut or other treatments that will make you feel confident and attractive. Though it can be a bit trickier to eat healthy on a budget, it can be done. Watch out for sales, and buy only what you think you will actually use. If it's too difficult for you to buy organic or diet food, just cut back on what you currently eat – everything in moderation!

When you take care of your appearance and your health, you become more attractive to your spouse. You also become happier and less stressed. As discussed earlier, couples may fall out of love because of the loss of physical attraction towards each other. If you have been in the relationship or marriage for a long time, chances are, you have been busy taking care of your partner or kids and have neglected yourself. You might have developed the habit of eating an unhealthy diet, and as a result, you have gained weight. If you take care of your appearance and health, you will be more confident, and you will be happier. When you are happier, you are less angry and frustrated, and you will have this positive energy that allows you to appreciate your partner more. You will also have all of the energy and vitality to bring back the passion and excitement in the relationship.

Acknowledge Your Needs, Emotions, and Preferences

In a relationship, it is important to communicate with your partner. Perhaps at this stage, you think that your spouse or partner should know everything about you. Your partner has been with you long enough, so he or she should know what makes you tick. However, this isn't possible.

Think about it this way; your partner has the responsibility of taking care of his or her emotions, preferences, and needs. Just like you, your partner has things in life that annoy, frustrate, or fill him or her with joy. As wonderful as it could be, your partner is not a mind reader. Even if the way you are feeling about something seems crystal clear, it's still important to talk about it. If your partner is on the same page as you, then great; if he or she is completely blindsided, it's good that you spoke up. If you have children or other responsibilities, these feelings and opinions could be even more buried due to necessity. Regardless, you must make an effort to take time to communicate. If you are unhappy or suffering, everyone else suffers, too.

It's also possible that your needs and preferences have changed since the beginning of your relationship. Maybe at first, you were looking for someone who could take you on fun dates or would spend time with you when it was convenient for both of your schedules. Now that the relationship is older, maybe you are looking for something more. Are you ready to make your relationship more serious? Do you need your partner or spouse to get a higher paying job so that he or she can take some of the burden of bills from you? You have to decide what it is that you need to keep you happy. This could include points made in previous sections of this chapter. Are you feeling stifled? Do you have dreams that you want to fulfill? Think about it, write them down, and find a way to organize what you desire out of your life and out of your relationship. Once you can come to terms with your stance on these issues, you can share them with your partner.

Arguments can be healthy. Meanwhile, bottling up your emotions can put pressure on you and can become too much if you keep them to yourself for too long. Not only that, but what couple truly agrees on everything all of the time? A relationship requires compromise, and it requires give and take. By no means should you or your partner be totally submissive to the other, but you should both be willing to make changes. This is why you need to communicate how you feel, even if it seems foolish. Maybe you won't agree, and maybe you will argue with each other, but it's important to be upfront with each other. By no means is it okay to be condescending or disrespectful to your partner; isn't it better to work things out between you? Talking about your feelings is a much better alternative to losing your relationship. You never know; your spouse or partner may be feeling the same way.

A great thing about discussing parts of your relationship is that they can bring you closer together. Once you tell your partner what you desire in the relationship, he or she may also share his or her own needs and preferences that you can be mindful of. You are also making an effort to strengthen the bond that you have. You are showing each other that you love each other and are willing to make things work. If your significant other sees that you love him or her, despite shortcomings or frustrations, he or she will be more likely to want to do the same for you. Also, if you show your partner that you care about yourself as much as you care about him or her, then your partner may follow your example and care for him or herself, too. Both of you can then be open, happy, and less stressed out. When you know what you want, everyone wins.

When you are in a relationship or marriage for a long time, you tend to keep your needs or even your opinions to yourself. Sometimes, you might hold everything inside so that you don't upset your spouse or partner. Maybe there are other commitments or responsibilities in your life that have pushed your feelings to the background. To show love for yourself, you have to be honest about how you feel about the relationship, including your frustrations. When you acknowledge your frustrations and communicate them to your partner or spouse respectfully and constructively, you become more open to your partner. Acknowledging your emotions is not only a sign of self-love, but it will also help you improve communication with your partner.

It is important to remember that you cannot fully love and accept your partner if you do not fully love and accept yourself first. When you are unhappy with yourself, it is often easier to be unhappy with your partner. When you love yourself, you become a happy person who has a lot to offer in a relationship. You have less emotional issues and baggage. Don't worry about being a nuisance, and do not assume that your significant other doesn't care. Your partner might be waiting for you to tell him or her how you feel or might have no idea that you are suffering inside. When you reclaim your identity by practicing self-love, it becomes easier for you to fall in love with your partner once again.

More Tips

Here are some other tips that will help you love yourself:

Understand Why You Love Yourself

You need to know how spectacular you are. When you look at yourself in the mirror, you need to be kind to yourself. What you see in the mirror is what everybody in the world sees, too. If you are disappointed in others, it could be a reflection of you being disappointed in yourself. When you accept others for who they are, you will accept yourself for who you are. The same can be said about potential. So, you get the idea. You need to show yourself some love so that you can show the people around you the same love.

Accept Yourself

This is very difficult for people to do. People always strive for perfection. They will do whatever they can to be perfect. When you do this, you lose yourself. So, it is a good idea to start by giving up on the idea of perfection and focusing on becoming your true self. When you do this, you will train your mind to love and understand life the way it is, rather than wanting it to be a certain way.

Stop Looking for Approval

Remember that you do not have to do what everybody else is doing. You have permission to do some things differently if you want to. You only have so much time on the planet, so why do you want to spend that time trying to please someone who does not care about you? Remember to focus on what you are doing today because you are exchanging a day of your life to do it. You never need permission from anybody else to live.

Stay Away from Negativity

It is better to be alone than to be in a relationship with the wrong person. You should never worry about people who do not care about you. You must know your worth. If you are in a relationship with someone who does not respect you, you have lost. Make sure that your friends always motivate, respect, and inspire you. The same goes for your partner, too. You should have a supportive circle of friends and family. Remember that you should always look for quality over quantity.

Forgive Yourself

You must get rid of negativity and bad thoughts. This is the only way you will learn to grow. It is okay to make bad choices, and it is perfectly okay to do badly. You are only human. Stop focusing only on the past. It is over, and there is nothing you can do to change it. You only need to focus on what you are doing now.

Make the Necessary Changes

Yes, some things would have made you very happy in the past. These things do not have to make you happy in the present, do they? This means that you do not have to stick with them forever. If you want to change your life, you need to do those things that you have not done in the past. When you do things differently, the output will be different. Get rid of the things that drain you, and move on to doing fun activities. Make sure that you choose activities that fulfill and empower you.

Embrace Your Mistakes

If you want to be successful, you need to fail, too. So, do not let the fear of making incorrect decisions prevent you from doing something new.

Show Gratitude

There are many things you will want, and you may not always get these things. You will not always be where you want to be, either. You, however, need to remember this: Many people can never not have what you have now. So, use that frustration, inconvenience, and pain to help motivate you. This is the only way you will do better. Remember that you control your happiness.

Perform an Activity That Makes You Happy

Gratifying exhaustion and empty fatigue are very different. Life is short, and you only live once. These may sound cliché, but it is the truth. Life is good when you make good decisions every day. These decisions should make you do something better in life. You need to care for yourself every day. Perform activities that you care about. What you need to understand is that there is nothing wrong with self-care. You cannot give someone what you do not have. Make sure to experience life the way you want to before you give life to others.

Explore Opportunities and Ideas

You should never let the fear of not knowing how things will end prevent you from doing something. The outcome of an action is indeed uncertain. Having said that, this uncertainty will lead you to new opportunities.

Be Honest

If you are not living a certain lifestyle, you cannot honestly talk about it. You do not need a life that can be made into a movie. You only need to live a genuine life. Always listen to your inner voice. You will be confident when you know what it is that you are doing, especially when you know that what you are doing is right for you.

Believe in Yourself

Everything is possible. You need to know what it is that you want, and claim that as a part of you. Remember to tell yourself that you are worthy of having everything you want.

Focus on Your Story

Do not read another person's story or watch it on video. You should focus on writing your own story. When you catch yourself comparing your life with another person's, you need to remind yourself that you have only seen what they want to show you. They have not told you the whole truth about their life.

Pay Attention to Your Life

One of the biggest gifts you can give yourself is always to be present. This is one of the greatest gifts you can give friends and family, too. What you need to understand is that your life is not about the memories you make between your birth and your death, but between this second and the next. We are indeed distracted on most occasions because of the devices in our hands. We need to remember to look up sometimes.

Do Not Be So Serious

Remember that self-pity leads to self-misery. You only pity yourself when you take life too seriously. If you take everything in your life seriously, you will fear any new step that you want to take. You should loosen up and laugh as much as you can. You should do this when things do not go as planned. People who have a sense of humor have a better sense of life, too. When you learn to laugh at your circumstances and yourself, you will have grown up.

Be Kind to Others

Remember that everything comes full circle. When you love yourself, you can show genuine love, care, and compassion towards others. You will learn to express yourself with confidence. You will be inclusive and forgiving. So, make sure that you understand other people before you judge them. You should also be thankful for rude people because they show you what you must not be.

Chapter Four: Nurture your Friendship

A person you like and enjoy spending time with is a friend. Your closest and dearest friend is your best friend. Friendship is the first step to creating any form of personal relationship. It's usually based on shared interests and a willingness to share all the joys and sorrows of life. The friend you are closest to is your best friend.

Importance of Friendship

How do you feel when you spend time with your friends? Do you feel relaxed, happy, and carefree? Friendship is one of the strongest bonds you can share with another person. Friendships are based on trust, honesty, love, and respect. The pillars of friendship are the same as the ones required for a successful relationship. There's a popular misconception that the lack of love is the leading cause of unhappy marriages. If you look at the issue, you will realize it is the lack of friendship, which causes unhappy marriages. Friendship is almost similar to maintaining a garden. You need to cultivate it. If you want the garden to flourish and thrive, there needs to be consistent effort and some love. All this needs to be done without having any expectations. It might sound too philosophical or even too good to be true. However, all this is true.

Do you believe you and your spouse are friends? Is it a good idea to be best friends with your partner? The answer to these questions differs from one person to another. Some believe it's better to have another individual as your best friend and not depend on your partner for friendship. Well, this seems to be a popular opinion. The ones who support this notion strongly believe that it is never wise to put all your eggs in the same basket. Well, they couldn't be more wrong. As it turns out, the basis of a successful marriage is friendship. It's not about putting your eggs in the same basket, but it's about finding another person who is always there for you.

If your partner is your soulmate, lover, and best friend, you don't have to look for anyone else ever again. One person fulfills all your needs, and it certainly doesn't get any better than this. When marriage is based on friendship, the entire relationship becomes more wonderful and fulfilling. That said, there are no specific rules about friendship, and there is no right or wrong. The only thing that matters is whether something works for you or not. If you are looking for ways to rekindle the love in your marriage and strengthen your bond, nurturing the friendship you share is quintessential.

Are you wondering why it is important to be friends with your partner? Here are some reasons that will certainly change your mind.

A Lifetime Together

Spending and sharing your life with someone you don't relate to, have a tough time understanding, or don't share an emotional bond with is difficult and unpleasant. This is one of the reasons why couples need to grasp the importance of friendship in a marriage. When you become best friends with your partner, you accept and love the person the way he or she is. You do this despite his or her good and bad points. Your ability to unconditionally accept your partner, and vice versa, increases with friendship. It also means it becomes easier to forgive each other for any small mistake or misunderstanding, and this strengthens your marriage. When you put all these factors together, it improves your ability to stay with each other. It's not just the bond that is strengthened but the health of the marriage improves, along with its duration.

Easy to Open Up

Have you ever noticed that it is quite easy to open up to your friends? Imagine how much easier it would be to open up to your partner if you both are friends? Friendship gives you a chance to be honest and open about yourself and everything associated with you. Friends don't judge one another, and the same translates into the relationship because of friendship. If you and your partner are open and honest, it increases the comfort you feel. These things, in turn, strengthen the emotional bond you share. It also acts as a foundation for an everlasting relationship based on mutual trust, love, and respect. If you have to walk on eggshells around your partner, it becomes stressful. If you constantly had to filter all your thoughts and emotions before expressing them, you can have a tough time being honest and open.

Sharing Life Experiences

Why should you and your partner be best friends? This is because you have to share a lot of life experiences. Friends are there for you through the good and bad times in life. The friendship in a marriage ensures that you and your partner are there for each other, regardless of the circumstances, situation, and obstacles that come along. When you start sharing all the small things in life, regardless of their triviality, and revel in these shared experiences, you get to know each other better. It also gives you a chance to learn from each other's experiences. Sharing life experiences is also a great way to strengthen the bond you both share and move forward in the right direction. It gives you better insight into each other's wants, preferences, and needs. A combination of these factors enriches your life and relationship.

Increases Enjoyment

Accepting each other's likes, dislikes, and opinions make things easier. Acceptance isn't the same as resignation. Acceptance stems from understanding and a willingness to see the person the way he or she is. This understanding makes the relationship more pleasant. Doing things for each other because you want to, instead of thinking of it as a chore, increases the enjoyment quotient in a marriage. It, in turn, increases your shared life experiences. Every little thing you say and do becomes the building block for something better. Anything that comes your way, whether it is good or bad, can be easily overcome.

Do Not Take Each Other for Granted

If you and your partner are best friends, it becomes easier to prioritize each other's needs and requirements. This kind of selflessness goes a long way in strengthening the bond you share. If you are more considerate of your partner, prioritizing each other's needs comes easily. It doesn't feel like a chore or an effort, and you need to do this consciously. Instead, you automatically understand that neither of you is supposed to take the other for granted. Once you start caring and being there for each other, it strengthens the security in a marriage. The feeling of safety and security that you will not be taken for granted gives you more freedom to explore yourself in the relationship you share. As mentioned in the previous chapter, safety and security are pillars of a happy and successful marriage.

Bliss, Peace, and Satisfaction

If two different individuals start living together, there will be ups and downs. There will be times when you both agree on everything and instances when it feels like neither of you can come to an understanding. Marriage includes the willingness to compromise, but this is not what it's all about. If you consider the points mentioned until now, you'll realize it becomes easier to view the situation from each other's perspective. This further strengthens the empathy, compassion, and love you feel. Love, empathy, and compassion are important for staying in sync in a marriage. Your marriage starts flourishing because of all the peace and satisfaction it brings with it. If, after every argument or minor disagreements, you and your partner start reevaluating the entire marriage itself, it brings a lot of discord and unhappiness. The ability to see each other's perspective makes it easier to understand where your partner is coming from. Making decisions becomes easier, and the sense of satisfaction you experience increases. Being friends with your partner is a great way to establish marital peace, bliss, and satisfaction.

Tips to Strengthen Your Friendship

Now that you are aware of the different benefits of friendship in a marriage, what do you feel? Loving and living with each other becomes easier with friendship. This might make you wonder what you can do to strengthen the friendship in your relationship. Well, you don't have to wonder because in this section, you will learn about simple tips you can use to strengthen your friendship.

Don't Be Controlling

If you want to grow closer to your spouse and become best friends, you should stop being controlling. Knowingly or unknowingly, partners tend to be controlling. Stop yourself from telling your partner what he or she is or is not supposed to do, especially in front of outsiders or friends. This can make your partner feel stifled in the relationship, and distance starts creeping in. If you or your partner don't say or do things because you believe the other person will not be appreciated, the chances of withdrawing from each other increase. Instead, allow your partner to do what he or she wants to do.

Remember that you and your partner are not single entities and will have differences in opinions, thoughts, beliefs, and feelings. As long as you both agree on the basic principles of a marriage, there is no need to control it. Even if there are instances when you believe you need to tell your partner what he or she is doing is wrong or what he or she can do better, talk to your partner in person. Avoid having such conversations in public; whether it's with your loved ones, family members, friends, or others. You need to keep in mind that you should be calm and composed while having such conversations and not say anything to make the other person feel guilty. Once you stop being controlling, the relationship will blossom and thrive. It gives you both the space required to explore yourself and your desire without any worries or judgment.

Personal Space

Every individual needs personal space, and when it is invaded, it creates feelings of suffocation. Being with each other and doing things together are not the same as spending every waking moment together. It is perfectly acceptable if you and your partner want to do different things. You don't have to prevent yourself from expressing your likes, dislikes, or desires merely because you want to be friends with your spouse. In a healthy marriage, a little space is more than important. It helps you to reconnect with yourself and gives you a chance to express your true self. Positive self-expression and acknowledgment of each other help lift an enormous burden from the marriage. The only thing you need to concentrate on is striking the perfect balance between your personal space and spending time with each other. You will learn more about all this in the subsequent chapters. For now, remember that a little me-time is healthy for your mental, physical, and emotional wellbeing, and it's also essential for the health of the marriage.

Start with Acceptance

If you cannot accept each other the way you are, it creates problems in a marriage. A relationship is not about perfection; instead, it's about accepting all imperfections and loving each other despite of them. If you keep pinpointing each other's flaws and imperfections, it quickly takes away the joy from the relationship. A simple realization you need to come to and accept is that nobody is perfect, and you cannot expect perfection from anyone, including yourself. Your partner likely does things that irritate or annoy you, which may include his or her behavior, quirks, or thinking process. Give your partner the benefit of the doubt and understand that he or she probably sees the same things in you, too. After all, the relationship is not a one-way street.

Once you start accepting your partner the way he or she is, loving your partner becomes easier. If you see things the way they are, living in the moment without unnecessary fears, worries, or expectations weighing down on you also becomes easy. Instead of worrying about the flaws or imperfections, concentrate on all the good in your life and relationship. If ten things annoy you about your partner, it's quite likely that several other things bring you joy. The next time you get annoyed, remind yourself of your partner's positive aspects, and it will make you feel light. You cannot be friends with anyone you don't accept. This is the same kind of acceptance you need to show each other in a marriage for it to thrive.

Support System

We all need a support system to get us through challenging times in life. This support system gives us not only the motivation and strength required to keep going in life but also advice in times of need. One of the simplest ways through which you can express your love for and acceptance of each other in a marriage is by being each other's support systems. Supporting your partner in his or her times of need is a great way to show you, love, understanding, and respect for the way he or she is.

Standing by your partner's side at all times and being a constant support system in his or her life will strengthen the marriage. It enhances not only the friendship you share but also the love. When things are going smoothly, it is easy to stand by your partner. The real test is when things don't turn out the way they are supposed to.

No Secrets

You cannot have any secrets in a friendship. Secrets quickly erode the trust in a relationship and allow unnecessary doubt and suspicion to creep in. If you want to be your partner's best friend, ensure your relationship is transparent. Transparency is not just about actions, but it's also about communication. Try to communicate as openly and honestly as you possibly can with your partner, and vice versa.

Communication is not just about talking, but it's also about listening. One person cannot keep talking while the other one always listens. The roles of speaker and listener need to be played by both the partners in a happy marriage. You wouldn't want to be friends with someone who keeps talking, would you? Likewise, you wouldn't want to be friends with someone who doesn't pay attention to the things you say.

Remember these two things when it comes to your marriage: It's always better to share facts and communicate about things the way they are. Hiding certain facts from each other because you believe the truth will hurt the other person is never a good idea. The thing with truth is that, sooner or later, it always comes out. It's better to be honest and share this information on your own instead of allowing your partner to find out from other sources.

The lack of secrets in a marriage brings the partners together. It also strengthens your friendship.

Mutual Trust

No relationship can exist without trust. Even a simple transaction, such as purchasing a new bag, involves a degree of trust. You trust the seller will give you the product you desire in exchange for the money you promised to pay. This is a simple act of trust. Yes, we might not have realized all this, but trust is important in every transaction and relationship. The same rule applies to your marriage. Trust your partner, have faith in him or her, and don't be possessive. It is okay to believe you belong to each other, but it doesn't mean you become controlling or possessive and jealous. There is no room for possessiveness in a healthy relationship. Trust is quite critical and fragile. All it takes is one wrong move, and trust will easily shatter. The best way to prevent this from happening is by openly communicating with each other.

Care and Love

We all have different priorities in life, and there is nothing wrong with that. The one thing you should always prioritize is your marriage and your partner. There is no way around it. By prioritizing, you are showing your love for your partner. Simple ways to make your partner feel loved and cared for are by taking care of each other, especially when your partner is not well. Try having at least one meal together every day, and learn to stand up for each other. It is okay to have disagreements, but you should always present a unified front. Any disagreements you have can be sorted through open communication. All the love you have for your partner doesn't matter if you cannot show it.

Speaking Out

We are all human beings, and the only way you can make others listen to you is by speaking out your heart and mind. Talk about your expectations, and don't worry about speaking out. If something bothers you, it's always better to talk it out instead of turning a blind eye towards it. It's quite easy to ignore things when you both are having a good time. However, these unpleasant memories will come to the forefront when things start unraveling. Moreover, if something bothers you right now but you don't talk about it and bring it up after a couple of months, it would make no sense. It can also surprise your partner because he or she wasn't aware of the problem. This is one of the reasons why honest communication is quite important in a marriage. Remember that even friends have disagreements, which are good for a healthy relationship.

For instance, if you are bothered that your partner doesn't help around the house as much as you would want him or her to, talk about it. If you keep doing everything on your own and after a couple of months, tell him or her, "You never do anything," your partner will be caught off-guard. Such behavior also makes the other person believe whatever he or she is doing is perfectly acceptable. If something isn't acceptable to you, talk about it. This is also a great way to implement your boundaries.

Respect

Always be mindful of what you say to your partner. It doesn't mean you need to think a hundred times before conveying your thoughts or feelings. Instead, it means communicating these thoughts or feelings positively. There is a difference between saying, "I wish you would help more around the house," and saying, "You never do anything." The thought you have conveyed is pretty much the same, but how you have delivered it also matters. If you are disrespectful towards each other, it quickly ruins any traces of friendship from the marriage and also weakens the bond you share. How do you want others to behave towards you? You want them to be respectful, considerate, and understanding. Remember these three things whenever you communicate with your partner. What you give is what you get, and a marriage is no exception. Don't put your partner down, and never be disrespectful to each other in front of others. If you invalidate your partner's feelings or are disrespectful to him or her in front of others, it quickly makes your partner feel devalued. It is okay to talk about any mistakes either of you make in private, but it is not up for an open discussion in front of family or friends.

Quality Time

The simplest way to strengthen the friendship you share with your partner is by spending quality time together. Whether it's going out for a walk, eating a meal together, or even watching a movie, spending time together matters a lot. Try doing activities you both enjoy. If you don't find any common activities, start cultivating new interests. If your partner likes something, you both could try that activity for one week, and then move on to something that you like the following week. A marriage is about compromises and understanding each other. Once you start experiencing things that your partner does, it creates more shared experiences and strengthens your understanding of each other. Don't get so overwhelmed by each other's lives that you forget about living life together.

Spending time apart is as important as spending time together. Always make space and room for each other in your life. Even if your days get hectic, having a meal together can work wonders for the relationship.

No Ego

There is no room for ego in any relationship. The best relationships are often ruined by ego. It is okay to make the first move. It is okay to apologize when you are wrong, and it is okay if your partner is upset. However, it is not okay to avoid doing these things because of ego. Learning to let go is an important part of overcoming any ego you have. If there is an argument, it's unimportant to identify who started it or why it started. Instead, the only thing that matters is how it ends. Arguments, fights, and disagreements are common. However, if such unpleasant circumstances are not dealt with properly, they chip away at the bond you share. Instead of dealing with the situation at hand, if you both indulge in a game of blame, it doesn't serve any purpose. Chances are, it merely worsens the situation.

Don't let your ego prevent you from accepting responsibility for your actions and mistakes and apologizing. Remember that your relationship is more important than all this. If you unconditionally love your partner, there is no room for ego. At times, all it takes is an honest apology to fix things and strengthen the relationship. Even after a fight, find it within yourself to go and hug your partner and tell him or her that you love him or her despite whatever happened. It also strengthens the security you both feel in the relationship while making each other feel appreciated and loved.

Love isn't just about saying, "I love you." This is an easy thing to do. However, showing you love your partner is more important. A silly fight is not a valid reason to end a good relationship. If it is your ego talking, then the silly fight will seem like a valid reason. Learning to identify when it is your ego at play increases your self-awareness. This kind of self-awareness reduces the chances of similar events reoccurring in the future.

Sacrifice and Compromise

No two individuals can agree on everything; it just isn't possible. Therefore, learning to compromise and make sacrifices is a part of every relationship. The same applies to marriage, too. The sacrifices and compromises you need to make aren't always about major decisions; it could be something as simple as watching a game on TV when your partner wants to watch a soap opera. When you are friends, these small adjustments don't seem like much. Learning to compromise also shows you understand and care for each other. Once again, there needs to be a give and take, and it isn't always about one partner giving up what he or she wants to please the other.

Equal Footing

A marriage is a partnership, and you both are equals. You are equal in every aspect, so always remember this when it comes to decisions. You cannot make decisions on behalf of your partner or make such decisions without considering your partner's opinion. You cannot decide on what's best for the other; you can only make suggestions. Never prevent your partner from speaking out, and don't hold back from expressing your opinions. However, while doing this, you need to play the role of a listener and an active observer.

If someone else is talking, ensure that you give this person all your attention, and concentrate on what he or she is saying. How can you respond to what the other person is saying if you haven't paid any attention? When you start listening to what the other person says, it becomes easier to understand where he or she is coming from. Doing this simple thing ensures that your partner feels like you are both equal. It, in turn, increases the respect you feel for each other. Listening carefully, acknowledging what your partner says, and respecting his or her wishes are simple ways through which equality can be maintained in any relationship.

Family Matters

Marriage isn't just about the individuals in the equation; there are several other parties involved. From friends to family members, learning to take an interest in each other's personal lives is important. After all, two families are coming together for marriage. Therefore, start making an effort to understand your partner's family, friends, and other individuals in your partner's life. When you start taking this interest, it automatically makes the other person feel valued and cherished. It, in turn, will bring you closer to each other. Imagine how stressful life would be if you constantly had to juggle between your family life and life with your partner. This stress can be easily eliminated by ensuring that you both are equally involved with each other's families.

Appreciation

Friends appreciate each other. It is quite easy to point out others' mistakes and flaws, but appreciating their efforts also matters. At times, all it takes is a simple gesture of gratitude to show your appreciation. If your partner cooks for you or makes the bed in the morning, don't forget to appreciate him or her. Appreciating your partner's good qualities makes it easier to overlook his or her mistakes and flaws. It not only brings you closer together but also improves your morale as a couple.

Strengthening the friendship in a marriage doesn't mean the partners do away with all their other relationships. You and your partner should maintain your respective friend circles. That said, you should consciously work on strengthening the friendship you share. This process cannot be completed overnight, and it requires patience, time, and effort. Once you are willing to do all this, it becomes easier. Strengthening friendship is also important for rekindling the love in your marriage. You will never get bored if you are married to your best friend!

Chapter Five: Take Your Commitment Seriously

Once you find someone you like, falling in love is quite easy. You then say, "I love you," after sharing a couple of good memories. The next logical step would seem like getting married. Getting married isn't difficult, but staying married is. It takes effort and commitment. Commitment is the promise to be there with each other through all the curveballs life throws. Commitment is the inherent desire to stand by each other. It starts with the basic desire to want to spend life together when it comes to marriage.

If you start a project at work, it needs to reach a logical conclusion. The project might seem easy initially, especially when things move smoothly. Then come the deadlines, disagreements, and changes. Going through all these things is important to complete the project. What keeps you going in such instances? It is your commitment to the project. Commitment is a promise. The same is essential in every marriage. A marriage without commitment can end easily.

Opposites attract, and even science backs this claim. Commitment is something that binds these opposites together. Think of it as the cement holding together the blocks of your marriage. In a relationship, commitment isn't just about the present but the future, too. It's a promise that despite whatever happens in life, the partners in a relationship will be together. In this section, you will learn about the importance of marital commitment, different levels of commitment, and tips to strengthen this commitment.

Sofia Price

Importance of Commitment

Do you remember your marital vows? These vows were promises you made to each other. They signify your commitment to one another. A wonderful thing about marriage is that you have chosen someone you want to spend your life with, and guess what? The other person has chosen you, too! Every couple starts a relationship to stay together forever. Who wouldn't want the happily ever after promised by romantic movies? We all do. So, what happens, and why do couples decide to end their relationships? The answer is simple: life happens. Things start getting difficult, the real struggle starts, fights crop up, and it gets too hard to live together. Once you make up your mind about who you are committed to, it's essential that you follow through.

Commitment in a relationship isn't about losing yourself or your identity. It doesn't mean you need to love yourself less to be more committed to the relationship. Instead, it's about staying together no matter what happens. It's about teamwork and honest communication. Commitment is so much more than an engagement ring, and it's certainly not defined by your wedding band.

Commitment is the inherent belief about the permanence of your relationship, and it acts like a life jacket that keeps you both afloat. With commitment comes the understanding that staying together matters more than your individual needs. If there is no commitment in the relationship, trust and intimacy will slowly go away. Commitment is like the thread that weaves together the fabric of a marriage. It holds your relationship together, even when things get tough. Living together is quite easy when everything is hunky-dory. It gets difficult only when things don't play out the way you imagined.

What happens when your expectations don't materialize? In such situations, it is sheer commitment that keeps you both together. There needs to be mutual commitment in a relationship. Commitment helps strengthen your love, and it also acts as a safety net that protects your marriage. It allows both partners to grow and mature while increasing the love and intimacy you share. Initially, marital life can look quite exciting and enticing. With time, this excitement slowly fades away, and the one thing that holds you together is commitment.

Now that you have found someone to live your life with and the other person has chosen you back, it's time to commit to each other. True love is difficult to find, and once you find it, it's worth fighting for with everything you have. Marriage is also a legally binding commitment to each other.

Levels of Commitment

We all know what commitment means, but not many know what it truly implies. Commitment is the decision to devote yourself to the relationship and consciously work on it. There are three levels of commitment at work when it comes to a healthy marriage.

Personal Commitment

This level of commitment stems from within. It is one's inherent desire to staying committed to the marriage. This is the essential "I want to" statement. Once you are personally committed to the relationship, staying together becomes easier. However, personal commitment isn't about one partner's willingness. It needs to be mutual and something both the partners desire.

"I love being committed to my partner."

"I want to be commitment to my marriage."

"I enjoy being married."

Moral Commitment

Moral commitment signifies all thoughts and statements about what one "ought to" do. Morals help us distinguish between right and wrong. A moral commitment is the desire to do the right thing. This level of commitment prompts you to say and think along the lines of:

"I made a commitment to my partner, and I will honor it."

"Staying married is the right thing to do."

Structural Commitment

Structural commitment is about what one must do. Those with this level of commitment might think the following:

"I have to stay in this relationship."

"There are external factors that are making me stay in this relationship."

External factors shouldn't influence a relationship, but at times, this can be helpful, too. For instance, some couples stay married for longer than expected and unknowingly rediscover the love they thought was lost. When you try for a while longer because of external factors, even if it is family or societal obligations, it gives your relationship a fighting chance.

At times, one level of commitment might sound more convincing than others, but a healthy and happy marriage requires all three levels of commitment. Take stock of your marriage, and analyze your levels of commitment. Here is a simple example to get a better understanding of commitment. Take a sheet of paper and tear it. Ripping it apart will be quite easy. Now, try tearing two sheets of paper. It probably takes more effort to shred it. If you had to tear three sheets of paper layered on top of each other, it would take significantly more effort to tear. Likewise, these three layers of commitment work together and strengthen the bond you share.

Tips to Strengthen Commitment

Do you think there's some scope for improvement in your marital commitment? If yes, here are some simple tips you can use.

Going All In

A true form of commitment in a relationship is when you and your partner decide to go all in. It's not just your words; even your thoughts and actions should show this commitment. In fact, this is one strategy all couples should live by every day.

Relationships take work, and there will be days when the struggle seems endless. There will be conflicts, and there will be problems. Once you decide to go all in, there is no backing out. If you start second-guessing yourself or doubting whether you did the right thing, it becomes confusing. If you truly love your partner and accept him or her the way he or she, it is worth all the effort it takes. Learn to be present in the relationship, live in the moment, and keep working hard. Learn to cherish every moment you spend with your partner, and live in those moments. Unless you live in the present, you cannot cherish all this.

If you are constantly worrying about the future or are living in the past, you forget about the present. The present is where life happens, and this is the time you get to spend with your partner. You cannot predict the future, and there is no point in living in the past. Work hard to create the kind of future you desire, and keep working for it. When you decide to go all in, you are thinking about yourself and your partner and the relationship. It gives you a chance to think of ways to improve your relationship's health and lessen any burden you feel.

Simply put, you need to express your love for your partner. It is important to show that you care. Actions certainly speak louder than words, but it doesn't mean you forget verbal communication. It is okay to do a lot of things that say you love your partner. Unless you explicitly stated at times, it doesn't help.

No Distractions

Start eliminating unnecessary temptations and distractions, and it will automatically strengthen your commitment to the relationship. Remember that cute guy who was glancing at you flirtatiously at the bar? Well, forget about him. Do you stay up late to talk to that one friend who keeps sending funny texts? It might not seem like much, but it is a slow killer. There are several temptations and vices, including minor distractions that can quickly but surely push partners apart.

Do you remember the previous point of going all in and staying in the moment? Getting rid of distractions and eliminating temptations are part of that. When you are truly committed to your partner, no one else really appeals to your heart or mind. You are unconditionally devoted to that person. Even if the room is full of attractive people, you only have eyes for your partner. This is the kind of commitment you need to work towards. Forget about your social media for a while, along with what your friends are doing. Instead, concentrate on the relationship and what you desire from it. If you constantly get distracted by different things in this world, it takes time away from your relationship. All this extra time, effort, and energy, which are going towards temptations and distractions, mean that you get to spend less time on your relationship and with your partner.

More Positivity

Do you and your partner have any inside jokes? Maybe it's the first awkward date you had or a funny encounter that is forever stamped in your memory. Well, hold on to those memories. Every funny instance you shared and every positive experience are part of your love journey. Hold on to these memories, and try to make even the negative ones seem funny. Do you remember that horrible fight you both had a few weeks, months, or years ago? Is it possible to put a positive spin on it? Are there any instances from that fight that make you laugh now?

Things can seem quite overwhelming in life, and unless you hold on to your humor, things get difficult. Whenever you feel down or low, think about all your positive shared experiences. Try to create more of such experiences – that trip you've been holding out on because it costs a few extra thousand dollars? Well, go for it. If not, now, then when? Consciously make an effort to create more positive experiences. When you share such experiences, it gives you a common ground. These are the fond memories you always look back on with a smile on your face.

Things That Matter

Never let spontaneity leave your relationship; whether it's an impromptu vacation, a long drive late at night, or a surprise breakfast in bed, spontaneity matters a lot. Spontaneity makes your relationship and the love you share for each other more special than they already are. All the spontaneous moments need to be cherished because these are the things that make every relationship wonderful.

While being spontaneous, take into consideration the things that matter the most to you. If you decide your relationship matters the most, you need to work towards it. This is where commitment steps into the picture. If you like fashion and your partner likes sports, look for activities you could do together. Even if you cannot find any common ground, try to take more interest in what the other person likes. By showing simple interests and likes and dislikes, you are conveying a loud and clear message: "I love you the way you are, and I enjoy spending time with you."

Partner's Perspective

Try to see your relationship from your partner's perspective. Whenever we look at things that happen in your life, we often view it from our perspective. Once you realize that everything can be viewed from multiple perspectives, it changes your entire outlook. To strengthen your commitment, there needs to be an inherent willingness in both the partners to understand each other's perspectives. Instead of getting stuck in your own head and viewing things from a single perspective, step into your partner's shoes. Once you do this, it becomes easier to understand what your partner needs, wants, and desires. This also gives you better insight into why your partner wants these things. Understanding your partner's needs, wants, and desires and the reasons for these things makes it easier to cater to them. To look at things from someone else's perspective, you need to keep an open mind and not let your ego step into the picture.

The simple tips given in this chapter will help strengthen the bond you share. Once you work on strengthening your commitment, safety, trust, and security increase. All these, in turn, increase shared intimacy. When all these factors are put together, they increase the love in the relationship.

Sofia Price

Chapter Six: Secrets of a Successful Marriage

Falling in love is quite easy, but keeping that love alive takes work. Jumping into a relationship is the easiest part. During the initial days, when everything is hunky-dory, the world seems like a better place. You start viewing everything through the rose-tinted glasses of love. However, once this honeymoon phase ends, that's when the real effort starts. Maintaining a healthy and strong relationship is seldom easy. Any effort you put in will certainly pay manifold. There is no secret formula you can use to have a successful marriage. Instead, it is about several little things that eventually add up. In this section, you will learn about the key aspects of a successful marriage.

Retain Your Independence

Retaining your independence is essential for leading a happy life. Whether you are in a relationship or not, you need to be independent. A lot of couples wrongly assume that marriage means letting go of one's independence. Instead, it is merely about leading a life together. If you want to be happy in your relationship, you must be happy with yourself. To do this, you must understand that your source of happiness lies in your hands. It is not dependent on someone else. If you keep looking for your happiness elsewhere, you can never truly be happy. Keep this in mind, and try to make a little time for yourself in the marriage. Just because you are married doesn't mean you and your partner are required to do everything together. If you wrongly believe this, you will both end up making each other miserable. Personal space is important in every aspect of your life, and a relationship is not an exception.

Do you remember the saying, "Absence makes the heart grow fonder?" Well, the saying is quite true. Take your "me time," and spend some time apart from each other. It doesn't mean you shouldn't meet for days on end. Instead, it merely means you should take at least an hour out of your daily routine to do things you enjoy. Spend time with your friends, go out, or indulge in any of your hobbies. In this time, you can reconnect and check in on your internal self. Once you are happy with yourself, you automatically bring happiness to those around you. Happiness is contagious. Therefore, you and your partner should work on making your own selves happy before you try to make each other happy.

Another great thing about retaining your independence is it gives you something to talk about at the end of the day. If you get too dependent on your partner, or vice versa, it can become suffocating for the other person. Remember that before you got into the relationship, you both had individual lives. Hold on to that sense of independence. You will learn more about loving yourself in the subsequent chapters.

Communicate in Each Other's Love Language

Love language encompasses all the different ways in which you communicate your love to your partner. When you not only understand but also successfully communicate in your partner's love language, he or she will feel loved, understood, and heard. It is also a great way to rekindle intimacy and romance in your relationship. When you finally start communicating on your partner's love language, it becomes easier to express your love for your partner, and he or she will appreciate it more. From surprising your partner with simple love notes and gifts and celebrating special occasions or doing chores around the house, there are different ways in which you can express your love. Follow the different tips discussed in the subsequent chapters about love languages, and implement them in your relationship today.

Learn to Listen

One sentence that almost every person in a relationship dreads is, "we need to talk." If you want to strengthen your marriage and make it happy, one of the simple secrets you need to concentrate on is creating an opportunity to communicate and converse with each other. Learning to listen is quite important. Unless you listen to the other person, how will you ever know what he or she is saying? If you hear the words merely to respond or react, it is not known as listening. Instead, keep an open mind and heart when your partner talks. Try to understand what your partner is saying, where he or she is coming from, and what he or she is feeling. Instead of concentrating on how you feel, when your partner talks, ensure your attention is focused only on him or her and nothing else. At times, all we need to do is merely listen to understand what the other person feels.

Accept Responsibility

When things go right or according to plan, it's quite easy to take credit. However, it is equally important to accept responsibility when you make a mistake. Accepting responsibility for your success and failure is an important trait that cannot be overlooked. In a marriage, there are two people involved, and both these people need to work together as a team to make it work. One partner cannot always be right while the other is wrong. Likewise, one partner shouldn't take credit when things go well and blame the other partner when things turn sour.

Even when you and your partner argue or have disagreements, take responsibility for your actions. Never shy away from accepting your mistakes. If you did or said something you shouldn't have, even if it weren't voluntary, accept your fair share of responsibility. Doing this shows your partner you care about what he or she feels and are sensitive to his or her needs. Good or bad, you are both in it for the long haul. It will do you both good to remember this simple vow.

Agree to Disagree

Regardless of how much you love each other, there will be topics you both cannot agree on. This is quite common, and it is not a sign of a bad relationship. In fact, in a healthy relationship, couples disagree, but they also know how to deal with such disagreements. Your attitude, personal beliefs, and opinions can be quite different on a variety of topics. All this is not only healthy but natural, too. A successful and loving marriage consists of partners who know how to deal with each other's disagreements and different views. After all, opposites do attract for a reason. Whenever you and your partner cannot agree on something, learn to agree to disagree and move on. A difference of opinions doesn't mean love is lacking. Instead of believing all this, learn to respect each other's point of view. Try to look for some humor whenever there is contention.

Just because you and your partner have different views, it doesn't mean one of you has to be right while the other is wrong. You can both be right in your ways, and you are both entitled to your own opinions. Don't let go of this knowledge, and learn to agree to disagree. Holding on to your own opinions and views is also a way of asserting your independence. However, learn when to let go. Not every discussion you have will end in an argument. Whenever there are disagreements, deal with them like adults. Don't allow your emotions to get the better of you. Reign in your emotions, and talk about whatever you want to. Be respectful to each other, regardless of how major the disagreement. Also, learn to understand that one of you doesn't always have to be right. The relationship is worth more to you both than being right.

Don't Take Each Other for Granted

Regardless of what you do, there is one thing no one should do in a relationship: take their relationship or their partner for granted. Becoming comfortable in the relationship is not the same as taking each other for granted. Once you're comfortable around each other, it means there are no inhibitions between you two. However, when you start taking each other for granted, it means you treat the relationship carelessly and indifferently.

In a marriage or any other long-term relationship, couples often reach a stage of complacency. This is the stage where we start lowering expectations and believe that whatever is there is good enough the way it is. During the initial stages of a relationship, couples go to great lengths to prove their love. After a period, all these things start decreasing. If you don't want love to wither away in your relationship, it's important not to become complacent. For instance, if you were to meet someone for a first date, you would try to look your best. Likewise, even if you've been married for over a decade, you should still dress up nicely whenever you go out for a date together.

If either of the partners feels like the other is taking him or her for granted, it will result in the buildup of negative feelings towards the other person. Regardless of what happens, you are supposed to respect and love your partner unconditionally. If there is any problem, it's always better to sort it out. Never make any assumptions, and try to do your best every single day. After all, a relationship is not a destination; it is an ongoing journey.

Intimacy Matters

No healthy or long-term relationship can survive without physical intimacy. Sex is not only a basic human need, but it is also important for a healthy marriage. Sex should not only be regular, but your sex life should be good, too. One of the most intimate ways in which a person can know another is through sexual intercourse. The simplest way to keep things interesting is by communicating. If you cannot have open or honest conversations with your partner about your sex life, it is time to improve your communication. From trying out role-playing to different sex positions and exploring different aspects of sex, there is a lot to do. Remember that a successful marriage always helps you achieve what you desire, regardless of whether it's in your professional life or the boudoir. You will learn more about stoking the sexual ambers of a relationship in the subsequent chapters.

Stay Romantic

In a happy and successful marriage, the partners look absolutely smitten with each other. Do you want to work on creating this kind of marriage? If yes, never forget to stay romantic. Never let romance get tired in your relationship. Romantic gestures don't have to be grand. You certainly don't have to serenade your partner or surprise him to her with elaborate or extravagant surprises and gifts. Instead, it's about simple gestures. Try to go a little old school with your idea of romance. Perhaps you could slip a love note before your partner goes to work in the morning, or maybe you can try purchasing a box of chocolates and some flowers for your ladylove. Surprise your partner with his or her favorite meal on the terrace, and watch the stars on a clear summer night. All it takes is a little romance to strengthen your relationship.

Incorporate Date Nights

A simple way to reclaim the romance and love in a relationship is by incorporating date nights. This is often overlooked by couples who have been together for a while. Regardless of what you do, it's important to spend some time with one another. You might go out for dinners with others, or attend commitments as a couple. However, all these things are not the same as going out for a date. A date night essentially refers to the time spent together without any distractions. During this period, ensure that you get rid of all distractions. Date nights don't necessarily have to be fancy. It could be something as simple as staying at home and eating pizza while watching a romantic movie. Maybe you could both cuddle under a blanket on a cozy night while listening to some soothing songs and sharing a bottle of wine.

From going out for a meal to staying indoors, there are a lot of options available. Regardless of what you do, ensure that you both concentrate only on each other.

Date nights can be romantic, thoughtful, quirky, fun, exciting, adventurous, and so on. The sky is the limit when it comes to a date night. Ensure that you have a date night at least once every week. Make it a weekly ritual, and don't avoid it. Regardless of all your other commitments, ensure that your date night is always a priority.

Search for Soft Emotions

Here's a simple example you should consider. Imagine you spend three hours in the kitchen cooking an elaborate meal. You set the table, dim the lights, and invite your partner to join you. Your partner sits down, places a portion on a plate, and starts eating. All this while, he or she hasn't even looked up from his or her mobile phone and seems to be engrossed while reading an article. You will probably showcase your irritation, anger, or annoyance. These three emotions are hard to express. However, most hard emotions are the manifestation of certain soft emotions. Perhaps you felt disappointed that your partner did not pay any attention to the meal you cooked and feel a little letdown. The soft emotion or the vulnerable emotion you experience here is a disappointment, and the hard emotion is anger. Instead of allowing harsh emotions to get the better of you, it's better to reach into the soft emotion.

Whenever a person feels angry, it's often because of another emotion, such as jealousy, sadness, or disappointment. Often, anger or other harsh emotions are used to disguise these softer emotions. It is okay to be vulnerable in front of your partner.

Love: Fall In Love Again

Instead of displaying an emotion that will trigger an argument or disrupt the environment at home, it's better to temper it in favor of your softer emotions. When you start expressing your real emotions, it becomes easier for your partner to relate to you. In the previous example, instead of shouting or getting upset with your partner, if you told him or her you were feeling disappointed that he or she isn't paying any attention to the meal you cooked, the overall effect of the conversation could be quite different.

Exchange Compliments

We all love compliments, and there isn't a single living soul who wouldn't love to be complimented. A simple compliment can light up anyone's day. Learn to compliment your partner. Make it a point to acknowledge your partner's positive attitudes and attributes. It's quite easy to pick on others and point out their weaknesses. However, doing all this adds no value to either of your lives. After a certain point, if the partners in a relationship stop complimenting each other or even acknowledging the other's positive attributes, the entire relationship takes on a negative hue.

When it comes to strengthening the bond you share with your partner, genuine compliments will go a long way. From complimenting your partner's smile and dressing sense and his or her kind gestures, there are many things to be thankful for. Compliments are also a great way to show your gratitude. For instance, if your partner always cooks your favorite meal on days when you are feeling down and low, it shows he or she cares and worries. The next time your partner does this, don't forget to compliment him or her. It could be something as simple as, "Honey, I love the meal you cooked," or, "thank you for worrying about me." When you shift your focus from negative attributes to positive ones, the happiness you also share increases.

Accept the Reality

All the romantic movies and fairytales we have been exposed to have unfortunately skewed our perception of reality. Marriages seldom turn out the way they are portrayed on the silver screen. The longer you hold on to this false sense of reality, the more difficult will things become. Instead, learn to accept reality. No marriage is perfect, and even the ones that last for decades have some flaws. What makes things beautiful is all their flaws. Marriage is a beautiful thing, but it certainly isn't effortless, and it cannot be perfect. Instead of comparing your relationship with all the fairytales you have read, it's better to look at things the way they are. If you don't do this, the only thing in store for you is a lot of disappointment. This disappointment can manifest itself as a set of ugly emotions that will harm the relationship you share with your partner. Instead of getting hurt and hurting your partner, let go of the fantasies, and live in the real world.

Accepting reality is an important aspect of life. It's not just in terms of your marriage but also your life in general. Things are the way they are. You can live with them, change them, or ignore them. If you believe there is scope for improvement, work on it. The sooner you accept this reality, the easier it is to become happy.

Never Mention the D Word

Regardless of what you do, never mention the D word in your relationship. Even during a heated argument, control your temper and don't mention the word divorce" or "separation." Never toss this word around casually. It has a lot of power, and it will invariably worsen any situation you are in. Breaking a relationship is quite easy and simple. However, if everyone were to stop trying at the first sign of trouble, there would be no happy relationships. Also, never use divorce or separation as a threat to get your way. If you want to be in a happy and successful relationship, you should act like a mature adult. Making threats doesn't solve any problem; it merely worsens the situation.

Stop Trying to Control

Don't try to control your partner. Whether you been together for five years or fifty, don't do this. It often happens that married people lose a sense of their former selves. If you forget that you and your partner are two separate individuals, one might likely try to control the other. People try to control their partners because of feelings of inadequacy, jealousy, or any other petty emotion. Never let these emotions get the better of you. The more you try to control someone, the more likely this person is to push you away. If you don't want this to happen in your marriage, stop being a control freak. Instead, as mentioned in the earlier points, remember that independence is very important for a successful marriage. You and your partner are independent entities. One shouldn't try to control the other. Instead, try to put your best foot forward, and be your best version if possible. If you think you are being controlled or you are the controlling one in the relationship, proactive therapy might help. You learn more about this in the subsequent chapters.

All the tips and steps given in this section are quite simple and practical. You don't have to do all these at once. Instead, start slowly, and discuss them with your partner. Once you are both on board with this idea, start implementing these key points. Even if it takes a lot of time, conscious effort, and patience, the results will truly be worth it. It seems like the glamorous actress Audrey Hepburn understood this idea, saying, "The best thing to hold on to in life is each other." So, hold on to your loved one, and work on the relationship.

Chapter Seven: Reminisce About the Happy Times

One of the things you can do to rekindle your love and affection for your partner is to take a trip down memory lane. You have to remember how it felt when you started the relationship. Remember the butterflies in your stomach. Remember how good your partner made you feel. Remember how your partner stood beside you through the good times and the bad.

To fall in love with your partner again, you need to spend five to ten minutes of your day thinking about the happy times. It may be that trip to Europe or funny moments you had. It may be the moment when your spouse made you laugh after a long and stressful day at work. It may be the moment when your partner took you to the most expensive restaurant or taught you how to drive or play golf. Do this as often as you can. Whenever you feel that you are bored in your relationship or you become frustrated with your partner, think about those happy times. Think about the times when you were still dating and you used to watch a lot of movies together and go out every Friday night. Think about the times when you went on a skiing or diving trip.

Most importantly, think about the times when you were still in the "honeymoon" stage when it seemed you couldn't get enough of each other. Remember the times when you had so much fun together and the times when you gazed into each other's eyes a lot. Take time to look at old photographs or old videos, and remember how those times felt. Doing this will instantly increase your fondness for your partner. It will help you focus more on the good times than the bad.

It would also help if you reminisced with your partner. Take time to open up and talk about a funny incident or a happy trip. You will surely have a few laughs together, and you will instantly feel more connected with each other.

Savoring the Past

According to a study performed at USC, it is a good idea to purchase a physical souvenir from any trip or memory you make. People will more happily talk about an experience when they look at this souvenir. For example, when you have guests over at home and you have a few souvenirs in your house, they will ask you about them. This will remind you about the memory. Let us assume that you are someone who does not believe in purchasing items to keep as souvenirs. How will you remember the event then? Let us look at some suggestions to help you remember your past:

Living in the Moment

People are always caught up with telling the world about their life. They want to use Snapchat or Instagram to show people how amazing their lives are. What they forget to do is live in the moment. Researchers have said that people forget that they are in a place. They are too busy looking for a way to capture picture-perfect moments that they forget to enjoy the place they are in. For example, when someone is in Paris, he or she may forget to enjoy the view from the Eiffel Tower. This person will, instead, look for the right spot to take a picture. He or she will not notice the people or things around him or her. The person

Love: Fall In Love Again

can only remember something from the picture on his or her phone.

This is something you and your partner should not do. Yes, you do need to have some pictures to remind you of the place, but sit together and think about the places that you have been to, and talk about how you felt when you visited those places.

Fairfield University conducted a study that showed that people remember more when they look at pictures. They want to record a moment and capture it in a photograph. What this actually does is that it damages your memories. People forget things about the place they were in when they only took pictures there. Researchers also found that people who took many pictures of the place they were in will remember very little about the visit.

If you think about it, you will remember something that happened to you in your childhood much better than something that happened a few weeks ago. If you meet a friend from school or camp, you can talk about anything under the sun because you remember what happened during those days. You do not need a picture to help you remember. When you do something next time – something that you think is memorable – make sure to create a memory for yourself and the people you are with. You should create a memory that very minute. You will probably enjoy doing that more because you will reap the benefits for years to come.

Recall the Good Times

Everybody makes a conscious decision and schedules their lives according to what they want or need. So, you must spend some time to revisit your memories. You and your partner could sit together and look at some old albums and pictures. You can also share some stories.

Another thing you could do is to practice journaling. You can keep a journal where you write about one thing that you loved about your day. Share these moments with your partner. Make sure you listen to him or her when he or she talks about memories, too.

Print Photos

Do you remember the time when you used to buy a roll of film and click photographs? You used to take the roll of film to the nearest store and print the photos. You would then spend your weekend scrapbooking. You should return to those roots. Always print pictures, and keep them. If you have a celebration at home or have gone on a trek, take a few pictures, and print them. This is a very inexpensive way to keep your memories alive. You can revisit these memories by looking at these photographs. Yes, this is counterintuitive to the first tip that I mentioned in this section. You need to spend some time in the present, but you also need to have some pictures to serve as a reminder.

When you and your partner want to reminisce about your wedding, you will pull out your album and look at the images. If you have an album from high school or college, just look at the pictures. If you have images of you and your partner, make sure to go through them. This is a great way to escape and remember your memories.

Relax

There is a lot of research that shows that it is important that you sleep enough to improve your memory. Let us break this down into simpler words. Have you watched the movie Inside Out? If you did not, let me tell you what it is about. The movie is about a girl named Riley and her emotion crew. When Riley goes to sleep, all her emotions work together and input the memories that she made throughout the day. These memories are stored in tiny marbles that are color-coded based on emotion. These marbles are sent through the vacuum into the long-term memory realm. This is a great way to learn about how human beings consolidate their memories.

During the slow-wave or deep sleep, your brain will cement the important memories that it will need to store for the long haul. Apart from exhaustion, you also have another reason to get to bed early.

Use Exercises Like Peak Moments

One exercise that you can do with your partner involves peak moments. When you perform this exercise, make sure both you and your partner have your eyes closed. When your eyes are closed, you should let all the peak moments flood through your mind. These moments should be those that were rewarding. When you remember all these rewards, you should both pick one moment, and dive deep into it. Ask yourselves what you felt when you were at that moment. See how your emotions were and also feel what the air was like. Within a few minutes, the two of you can understand what you were able to pull from experience. You will also understand what your partner values the most about his or her experiences. When you both focus on a memory, you will notice that you are focusing on your core values. You will probably be surprised that you are thinking about a specific aspect of the memory that you may never have thought about before. What you need to do is balance your present with your past.

Chapter Eight: The Appreciation Plan

If you have been in a relationship with your partner for a very long time, it likely means your partner has a lot of good qualities that you really appreciate. A long period of time may have passed or you've become so comfortable around each other that you may have begun to take these qualities for granted. Part of the Appreciation Plan is to remember all of the good things your partner has done for you. You have to remember your partner's good qualities and why you fell in love with him or her.

When you have lived with your partner or spouse for a long time, it is easy to notice his or her bad habits and qualities. You often magnify his r her quirks and mistakes while belittling his or her achievements and good qualities. You have to look past your spouse or partner's flaws and shortcomings for your relationship to work. If you want to fall in love with your partner all over again, you have to remember all of the qualities that made you fall in love with him or her in the first place. One way to ignite the fire in your relationship is to appreciate your partner.

Here's how you can show appreciation to your partner:

Remember All the Good Things that Your Partner Has Done for You

Remember how happy your partner made you feel when he or she completed errands for you, fixed your car, or raised funds so you could pursue your educational aspirations. Instead of focusing on what they your partner has done wrong in the relationship, focus on the things he or she did right. Instead of focusing on mistakes and failures, focus on achievements.

You have to find the silver lining. If your partner or spouse were selfish and negligent, you wouldn't be in a relationship with this person. What did your partner do to make you fall in love with him or her? It can be as simple as how he or she made you feel when you first met. Maybe your partner was funny or showed that he or she cared during a time in your life when it seemed like you were alone. Something about your partner lifted you up and made you excited about life. Is there anything from that time in your relationship that carries over to the present? Does your significant other still make you smile at times? If so, remember that this is something that has always made you attracted to your partner. There is no one else who can make you feel the same way, even if things might have changed since you first met.

Think back to why your partner did those great things for you. Maybe they took care of you because you were sick, or they allowed you to travel somewhere or have fun with your family or friends. Your spouse or partner cares about you and would not look after you, work for you, or spend his or her money if what he or she felt was not genuine. Do you feel more loved by your partner when he or she does those things for you? If so, you must look at your life at the moment and find ways that your partner is trying to please you now, and understand they do care.

Maybe these good things don't happen as often as they used to. You both may have other responsibilities, such as children that you are focusing on pleasing. Maybe your financial situation has changed with the purchase of a home or a vehicle, and what your partner was able to provide for you is no longer possible. There is even the chance that you and your partner have been together for so long that you aren't even aware of the positive things that he or she does for you anymore. It's important to spend more time focusing on the positives. Even if it's not as often as you would like, if your spouse or partner still occasionally does something nice for you, you need to appreciate his or her effort, and don't let it get taken for granted. Even if your partner isn't perfect, you must let the good outweigh the bad if you want your relationship to remain strong.

Write Down All the Qualities that You Like about Your Partner

Your partner might frustrate and even annoy you at times, but he or she has redeemable qualities. There are things about your partner that make your relationship worth fighting for. You need to think about the qualities he or she has that make you happy and make you love him or her. This is not something that can necessarily be achieved in a few minutes. You need to think about everything that you like about your spouse or partner.

Do you like your partner because of his or her appearance? Is he or she caring, honest, and loyal? Do you like your partner because he or she is hardworking, intelligent, or funny? Do you like your partner because he or she pays attention to what you need and want in life? Write down ALL of the qualities you like. Take time to remember every single quality. Make sure you do not miss anything.

Once you have made your list, go back and look at the qualities that you listed. Now that you have identified what you like about your partner, you need to support your choice. Give specific examples as to why these qualities make you love your spouse or partner. Did you write down that you think he or she is loving and that every day, when you get home from work, your partner hugs you and asks you about your day? Did you say that your partner or spouse was cheerful because no matter how bad a day either of you have, he or she always makes sure to find a positive spin to it? Do you like your spouse because of his or her stunning blue eyes that make you a bit envious because your eyes are a common brown color? Not only is it important for you to admit why you like certain aspects of your significant other, but you must know why you feel that way as well. This will make it easier for you to remember why you are in a relationship with your partner, especially when times get tough.

Read the List

Once you have listed all of the qualities of your partner that you really like, take the time to read the list. Read this as often as you can. Whenever you feel bored or frustrated, take out the list and read it. If you and your significant other argue, it is also a good opportunity to look at this list as well. This will help you remember why you are in the relationship in the first place. This will also reignite the feelings and passion that you have for your partner. You will instantly realize why you fell in love with this person. This will help you fall in love with your partner once again.

The list should be a constant reminder that your spouse or partner is worth fighting for. The list you made is not empty; the person you fell in love with is still important to you. Not only should this list make you fall in love with your partner, but it should also be a testament as to why you chose to start your relationship. If there is nothing positive about your partner, you would not have pursued the relationship in the first place.

The list doesn't have to be completed in one sitting either. You can write down more qualities as you remember them. Better yet, you can write down new reasons why you are attracted to your spouse or partner as you discover them. If you are paying attention to your partner, you may discover new things about him or her that you didn't realize before.

Share the List with Your Partner or Spouse

When you are comfortable with what you have written about your partner or spouse, it's important to let him or her know how you feel. Maybe your partner noticed that the relationship has fizzled out and are concerned. Sharing your list with your partner is a great way to affirm how you are feeling and put your significant other at ease.

Tell your partner how much you appreciate his or her good qualities. Tell your partner how handsome or pretty you think he or she is or how much you appreciate all of the hard work that he or she has done for your family. You could tell your partner about the positive qualities that he or she has that you wished you had. It could be the physical attributes that you wish you possessed, or you could also tell your partner that you wish you had a strong sense of family or were as comforting as he or she is. Make sure that you give the reasoning behind your list of positive qualities. This will show your partner or spouse why you fell in love with him or her and why you still continue to love him or her despite the difficult times.

Sharing your list with your partner or spouse can be positive in the sense of letting him or her know that you truly remember why you fell in love. It could encourage your partner to open up to you and make a list of his or her own. Your partner could rediscover all of the reasons why he or she fell in love with you, and it could rekindle what is still between the two of you. It will also allow your significant other to think about your positive traits when he or she feels frustrated or annoyed. Finally, sharing your feelings for one another can hopefully get you talking about other aspects of your relationship and having open lines of communication more often. It's easier to be open about your feelings when you both feel that you can do it comfortably.

Silence the Critic Within You and Affirm Your Partner Often

Sometimes, we fall into a trap where it's easy to place the blame on your partner or spouse, even for the most mundane of tasks. You assume that they should know your expectations. You feel like they should be aware of how you want something done, whether it's work around the house or remembering that you wanted to do something fun this weekend. You forget all about the positive things you wrote about your partner.

As much as possible, avoid criticizing your partner. You have to watch your thoughts and your words. If you think negative thoughts about your partner, immediately replace that thought with a positive one. The less you think negatively about your partner, the less you will be tempted to say your thoughts out loud. If you are on the verge of saying something hurtful or negative to your partner, stop yourself. Think of how hurt you would be if your partner said something hurtful to you. When you stop being critical of your partner, your partner will also eventually become less critical of you. Say affirmations to your partner often. Let him or her know how great he or she is with the kids or how great he or she is at their job. It's easy to dwell on the things that you don't like and the things that go wrong but don't fall into the trap. There are books and people everywhere that believe in the power of positive thinking. If you believe in your partner – if you truly believe that your relationship can be saved – then the power of positivity can make those thoughts become a reality. So, when in doubt, visualize yourself and your relationship as a happy place.

Never underestimate the power of appreciation. Appreciation is a powerful language of love that can heal all wounds and repair broken relationships. Yes, you may be unhappy about certain aspects of your relationship or certain things that your spouse or partner does, but if you let your partner know that you appreciate him or her regardless, your significant other will know that you care. A simple compliment or remark could get your partner to try that much harder to please you. Think of that when you want so desperately to tear your partner down for doing something wrong, and instead, reward your partner for the good, and try to take the not so good in stride.

Sofia Price

Chapter Nine: Rekindle the Spark

If you feel that the spark is gone or your interest in and attraction to your partner is dwindling, it is most likely that you do not have enough fun together, or you do not have enough time for each other.

There are many ways that you can bring the fun back into the relationship, regardless of your financial situation or schedule. Here are the steps on how you can bring back the lost spark in your relationship.

It's a Date!

One of the ways to reawaken the spark and passion in your relationship is to schedule a date night every week. Leave the kids with a babysitter or a family member, and go out to some fancy restaurant, or watch a movie together. You could also watch a sporting event, go to a concert, or watch a play. There are countless places you could go, and part of the fun could be in taking turns picking a new place for your date night each week.

Make sure to put in extra effort to look good for your partner. Wear something you don't wear every day, and try to make this night of the week a special occasion. Act like the relationship is still new. You could try to remember and revisit all of the places you and your significant other would go when you were first dating, or you could pretend that you are brand new to the scene and find new places to call your favorites.

During your date nights, try your best not to talk about the kids, money, or problems in your relationship. Forget your responsibilities or even who you are outside of the evening. Just have fun, talk about your interests, your hobbies, and your dreams. This can be a chance for you to rediscover each other. You may have forgotten all of the things that made you and your partner attracted to each other, or in the business that is day-to-day life, you or your partner may have new dreams or aspirations. It's a great way to learn more about the other, without interruptions or daily distractions, such as television, phone calls, or other things.

Check-In

All too often, life gets in the way of our relationships. Now that you are committed to each other and the newness of the relationship might have worn off, you don't bother with checking in with your partner. You probably do this unintentionally; you know your partner is just as busy as you and that he or she will be there when you get to him or her eventually.

If love is already fading away, it is most likely that you and your partner have been taking each other for granted. Even though you know that your partner will be there when you get home, it's still important to touch base with him or her. Take time to ask your partner how his or her day was. Take time to ask if he or she has already eaten lunch, just like you did when the relationship was still new. It could be as simple as letting your partner know that you love him or her and that you are thinking of him or her.

Also, let your partner know what you have been up to. Your partner is probably just as curious to know how your day is going as you are about his or her day. Don't worry if what you have to say seems trivial. Your partner or spouse will be happy to hear from you, and if you are happy and excited about what's going on in your life, he or she will be, too. Anything you have to say is helpful in keeping your relationship strong, and your significant other will appreciate that you include him or her.

When you are traveling alone somewhere, send a text message to your partner, letting him or her know that your plane has already landed or you have already checked in to a hotel. Not only will this let your partner know that you are safe, but this will let your partner know that he or she is an important part of your life. Your partner will feel loved and remember all of the good reasons as to why your relationship has made it this far. He or she will also be more inclined to check in with you, whether he or she are responding to a message that you sent or sharing his or her own news throughout the day. Communication is powerful, and any communication between the two of you will keep your relationship open and stronger than ever before.

Spend More Time Together

When you have lived together for quite a while, you often spend your nights not talking to each other. You may spend an hour web browsing while your partner is reading a book or watching TV on his or her own. Before going to sleep at night, spend some quality time together. While you might think that you're still together in the same room, it's not enough. Pick a TV show you and your partner both enjoy, and commit to only watching this show together. You can talk about what happened and predict what is going to happen next. Not only will it have you spending time together and bonding, but it can also open the door to get you communicating more than if you were on the computer, with your partner watching television alone. If you can't agree on a TV show, there could be another activity you could do together. Maybe you could read before bed and talk about what's going on in the story. It doesn't even have to be the same book. You could take turns talking about what's going on in your separate novels.

If finding quality time together before bed doesn't work for you, there are other times of the day where you can spend time together. Are you both on the competitive side? There is a whole variety of things that you could do together. You could play video games; maybe shooting at each other in an alternate reality could get some of your frustrations out while having fun at the same time. There is also a variety of games out there that require you to be actively involved and could have both of you up and moving. If virtual reality isn't your thing, there are board games and hundreds of other games that can be carried out with a simple pack of playing cards.

You can bond while playing other games, too. How about games that get you outside or away from home altogether? Play a game of one-on-one basketball together or Frisbee in your backyard. If you are up for an adventure that could be incorporated into a date night, bowling and billiards can be an inexpensive way to have fun. Plus, some healthy competition can ignite a spark between you and your partner. Being playful has its benefits.

Sometimes, it's better to bond in different ways. Go for a walk around your neighborhood, and talk about your day. Make time to sit on your porch or deck, and talk about something fun you'd like to do sometime in the future. Run out and get a coffee, and just sit in your car and talk. There are infinite possibilities for you and your partner to spend time together that don't cost a lot and don't take away from the other responsibilities you may already have. When you take the time to be together, you will rediscover all the wonderful qualities your partner or spouse has, and you will want to spend even more time with him or her.

Be Affectionate toward Your Partner, Both Physically and Verbally

Everyone needs to feel affection. To some people, it might be as simple as being verbally kind to his or her spouse or partner. However, some people crave affection like air or the food they eat. Think for a minute: Is your spouse or partner one of these people?

Do not be afraid or reluctant to have a term of endearment for your spouse. Call him or her "honey," "baby," or "sweetheart." Your partner will let you know which names he or she likes or prefers. Some people end up calling their significant other by their pet name more than their given name. Try it, and see what happens. Say "I love you" often, and say "Thank you" whenever your partner gives you a gift, says kind words to you, or does something really special for you. That doesn't mean that you can't say it over something simple, such as when your partner helps you with a day-to-day task like making dinner or taking out the trash. Telling your significant other that you love him or her at a moment like this also shows your partner that you appreciate everything that he or she does for you.

The words "I love you" should not be used loosely as a script to end a phone call. It also shouldn't be insincere. When you tell your partner or your spouse that you love him or her, make sure it is at a time that you truly mean it. Say it at the most unexpected times. Did he or she tell a joke that made you laugh to the point of tears? Is he or she doing something that makes him or her look attractive without doing anything special at all? Let your partner know. He or she will surely appreciate it. When having dinner or watching TV, tell your spouse how amazing and wonderful he or she is and how thankful you are that he or she is your partner. This could be the perfect time to tell your partner some of the things you wrote about him or her on your list of best qualities. Give at least one or two compliments each day. Don't worry if your spouse or partner doesn't believe you. Sometimes, people have trouble seeing themselves from someone else's point of view that is different from their own.

Nevertheless, a sincere compliment will surely make your partner's day. If you get into this habit, it could encourage your spouse or partner to think about how he or she shows you affection. If you take the lead, it will trigger your partner to reciprocate the use of terms of endearment, saying I love you, and trying to make you feel positive as well. Being verbally affectionate is also important because it will give your significant other self-esteem that you, in turn, will receive when your partner or spouse says kind things to you.

Just like people need to hear endearments, it is also necessary to show your affection to your partner by using the sense of touch. Do you remember how excited you would get when you would hold your partner's hand or kiss your partner back when you first met? Hug your partner often, or hold his or her hands like you did when the relationship was still new. Put your hand around your partner's shoulders or squeeze his or her hands. When you touch your partner often, your affection for him or her will surely skyrocket, and it will feel like you are in a new relationship again.

Physical touch can help your partner or spouse deal with various emotions and situations. If your partner is upset, an embrace

Love: Fall In Love Again

can comfort him or her. If your partner is nervous about something, squeezing his or her hand can provide him or her the strength to know that he or she has your support. An embrace or kiss can even be an affirmation of your love. If you find that your relationship is struggling and your partner or spouse seems concerned that you might want to end things, show him or her that you still care. It's an old and often used expression, but "actions speak louder than words." Hold your partner tightly, and let him or her know that you are there for him or her. These gestures may seem meaningless or unnecessary, but it is important to show your partner that you enjoy being near him or her. It will put your partner at ease and encourage him or her to want to make the same gestures for you. Once you can share these moments together, other aspects of your relationship will be even easier to improve. If you are not sure if your spouse or partner wants your touch, the easiest thing to do is to ask. If you are both open with each other and know what your wants and needs are, being affectionate towards one another will be easy and something that you look forward to.

Share New and Exciting Experiences

One of the great things about a new relationship is all of the "firsts" you have together. You never forget where you first met, the first place you went on a date, the first time you took a long drive in the middle of the night, or how you felt the first time you kissed. The relationship was and still is an adventure, and as you are in the middle of it, remember the times when you felt excited and alive and look forward to more.

If you want to rekindle your relationship and fall in love with your partner all over again, you have to share new and fun experiences. You can train for and run a marathon together or go skydiving. You can also go on a road trip or travel to another country. You will surely have a good time together, and you will definitely enjoy each other's company. Plus, when you get home, there is something new to talk about. You will surely share a few laughs with your partner when you recall these experiences.

Go out there and create new firsts; step out of your comfort zone. It might be scary or difficult at first, but who better to try new things with than your significant other? Try a new type of cuisine that has always interested you but were always too cautious about trying. Search for the best ice cream in your town and the surrounding area. Make it as random or fun as the two of you want. Go to a concert that one or both of you have always wanted to see. Does one of you like to read? Go to the local bookstore, or get out and discover a new favorite family-fun establishment. Research the natural landmarks in your area, and explore some new places. Find new favorites that you will want to revisit. It will make for a great story and a fun weekend.

You don't need to recreate the exact mood or feeling from the beginning of your relationship. That might only add to the frustration that you and your partner are dealing with. What you want to recall are the feelings of closeness or how you looked forward to that time together. You should be excited to go off and discover new things in the world while learning things about each other at the same time. This is the perfect time to find new interests and attributes that can make you more alluring to your partner. If he or she looks forward to trying new things with you, how can you not be excited and more appreciative of being around your partner?

Be Kind

Always choose kindness over anger and hatred. Be nice and supportive of your partner. If your partner shows up late for dinner because he or she had a long meeting, do not nag or become annoyed. Show kindness instead. Say something like, "We've saved your favorite dish for you as you may be hungry because of that long meeting." Also important is that when you are saying something, watch your tone. Most people fight not because of the words that were said, but how those words were said.

It's easy, in the midst of your stress and frustration, to forget this and lash out at your partner. Whether it is truly his or her fault or you are taking out the anger you feel because of someone else on your partner, try your hardest to stop yourself. While it might make you feel better to purge your emotions, how would you feel if someone was yelling or being unkind to you? No one likes getting yelled at, and you must think of that when you are with your spouse or partner.

There may be times when being kind is difficult. Maybe your spouse doesn't approve of something that you do that makes you happy. Maybe your partner can't understand why you need to do it when there are more important things going on in your life. It's possible that your partner feels that he or she is more important than whatever it is that occupies your time. If your partner is bitter and nasty towards you, you can feel like the best defense is being equally spiteful. Don't do it. Take the high road.

Talk to your partner, find out why he or she is truly upset, and then see if there is a compromise that can be made. It's not necessarily about each of you getting your own way but meeting somewhere in the middle. This shows that you are listening to your partner's opinion while not giving up your own. Even more important is the fact that you came to this conclusion while being kind. A lot can be accomplished when you aren't vindictive.

When you are kind to your spouse or partner, it's contagious. Your partner will want to do the same for you, even when he or she might be mad or frustrated with you. When you want to vent about something that is bothering you, your partner will listen without making you feel bad. Showing each other kindness will let your partner know that you care. Think of how you used to act when you and your significant other first got together. You would never have dreamt of hurting your partner's feelings. That should never change.

Listen

Take time to really listen to what your partner is saying. Let your partner talk about his or her job, interests, or opinion about current news and events, and truly listen and pay attention. Even if you are not interested in what your partner wants to talk about, you must listen and give some input anyway. It will mean a lot to your partner for you to hear what he or she has to say about a topic, even if it's something that you aren't crazy about.

Sometimes, it may seem like you and your partner have exhausted what you can talk about. You know everything about the other, or you've heard the same stories so many times that you could tell them on your partner's behalf. As frustrating as this might be, don't get mad at your partner. Think of it this way; your partner keeps on telling you that story for a reason. Either it's extremely important to your partner, or he or she thinks you like it. Regardless of the reason, make sure that you

Love: Fall In Love Again

are appreciative even when you remind your partner that you have heard it before.

One important communication skill needed in a relationship is listening – active listening. It can become easy to "tune out" your partner. Sometimes, you become so distracted with your own life that you don't always listen. Your spouse or partner may feel like you don't appreciate him or her if you have a long conversation and, halfway through, you have no idea what he or she is talking about. Try your best to truly listen. Cut out the distractions. If your partner is trying to talk to you while your favorite TV show is on, it's probably not going to end well. Turn it off, and listen to the words your partner is trying to convey to you.

Another important part of active listening is not just hearing what is being said, but looking at your partner's body language. If your partner is telling you that he or she is not upset about something, but his or her body language is telling you otherwise, you might want to voice your concerns.

Finally, a great way to let your partner know that you are truly listening is providing feedback. As your partner speaks with you, ask questions about what he or she shared, and give advice. Whether he or she is legitimately concerned about something or just telling you about his or her day, make sure that you are listening intently to everything that your partner says. Your partner will appreciate that you care about what he or she has to say. It also goes along with the idea of being open with one another. If your partner truly feels like you are listening, he or she will want to talk to you about other things, including your relationship.

Sofia Price

Surprise Your Partner Often

Do you remember the time in your relationship when you used to surprise each other with gifts and did it often? If you want to rekindle the spark in your relationship, spice things up by giving surprise gifts or taking your partner on a surprise trip. Surprises have a certain power that spices up a boring and predictable relationship.

Sometimes, a surprise doesn't have to be big or extravagant. Something as simple as your partner coming home to a clean house or his or her favorite meal is a great way to start surprising your spouse or partner. You could make your partner's favorite meal or take him or her to his or her favorite restaurant. Whatever you decide to do, think of how your significant other will appreciate it.

Find a weekend that your partner is free from other obligations, and go away on a surprise mini vacation. You could tell your spouse or partner the destination right before you leave, or you could keep it a secret and get in the car for what seems like a random errand and just start driving to the destination. Think of how excited your partner will be to go somewhere and how much you planned this for him or her.

Think back to the holidays that you spent with your spouse or partner. Do you remember how nice it felt to get gifts from your partner and how great it felt to give him or her a gift in return? Surprise gifts are just as nice because not only are you getting the satisfaction of making your partner happy, but you have the bonus of your partner or spouse completely not expecting it and being that much more appreciative because of that. The gift doesn't have to be expensive; something as simple as flowers or a thoughtful card can be a nice enough gesture. If you want to really wow your partner or spouse, give him or her something

Love: Fall In Love Again

that he or she has been eyeing for a long time or something that you know your partner really wants but would never buy. Your partner will fall in love with you all over again for being so thoughtful and kind and for listening to his or her interests.

A great way to surprise your partner or spouse is to spend quality time with him or her doing something he or she really enjoys. Is your partner a tennis player? Instead of going to the local court, you could take your partner somewhere special to play, or you could watch a tournament when it's held nearby. Does your partner love a certain TV show, movie, or another fandom? You could have a marathon party, complete with food and drink, or you could even surprise your partner by taking him or her to a convention or other event. Take your partner on a surprise hike if he or she likes the great outdoors. Even better, you could spend your quality time together while helping a great cause. Is your partner or spouse an animal partner? If so, you could spend some time at your local shelter without letting your partner know ahead of time. Go to a fundraiser; if it's something that you can do while surprising your spouse or partner at the same time, it's a great idea.

To rekindle the spark in your relationship, you have to act like you are in a new relationship again. You have to pay attention to your spouse or partner. You have to make time for your partner and open up your communication lines. You have to do those little things that you used to do when the relationship was still new. Relationships take work and need constant maintenance. You and your partner have to be willing to take the time to fix things and remember why you fell in love in the first place. When you do the things you used to do when you were still developing your feelings and affection for your partner, you will slowly fall in love with him or her once again.

Don't Go to Bed Angry

Fights happen, and arguments can sometimes be healthy. However, when you and your partner get into a disagreement, make sure that you work it out and clear the air before you go to sleep that night. It's not good for hurt feelings to fester for longer than they need to. That can lead to resentment and have the negative aspects of the relationship kept in the forefront of your mind. Be open with each other; make sure that you are being honest with what is upsetting you, but also make sure that you are listening to what your partner or spouse is saying. Many disagreements are misunderstandings, and talking things out instead of stomping off to your room and closing the door can make sure you understand each other better. It will encourage you to be mindful of what your partner or spouse is feeling.

Finally, make sure that you apologize. Whether or not you started the argument, before you fall asleep, make sure that you both say that you are sorry for hurting the other's feelings. This way, there is no room for resentment to creep in. You let your feelings out. You may have both gotten emotional or said things that you didn't mean, but now, it's over, and you can move on to tomorrow. Apologizing shows that you care about your significant other's feelings and that you don't want to see him or her hurt. Maybe you are not ready to put whatever angered you in the past just yet, but this way, you are still showing your spouse or partner that you love him or her anyway.

The more you show your partner that you care for him or her even when times are rough, the more it will prove that your love for your partner is strong and unyielding. If your partner feels that security, he or she will be able to love you back just as fiercely.

Remember Why You Fell in Love in the First Place

With jobs, children, responsibilities, and other distractions, it is easy for your relationship to take a backseat to everything else. If you find that your marriage or relationship is becoming dull, think back to what caused you to fall in love with your partner. Think about what made you notice him or her to begin with and how the two of you became a couple. Having happy memories about the birth of your relationship can get you recalling other important events as well.

Think about your first holidays together or meeting each other's parents for the first time. Can you remember where you were when your partner told you that he or she loved you for the first time? If you are married, do you remember exactly where you were when your partner proposed? Can you remember how you felt on your wedding day? If you find yourself feeling warm, happy, and overwhelmed with emotion at these memories, that's a good thing. That means that the love you felt for your partner is still there; you have to find a way to let it out and show your partner how he or she makes you feel.

This is the perfect opportunity to share your feelings with your spouse or partner. It could be as simple as reminiscing before you go to bed at night or talking about the best parts of your relationship over dinner. It can get you both talking and feeling nostalgic about a fantastic part of your life. Maybe at the beginning of your relationship, you would go for walks late at night or frequent a coffee shop that had fantastic drinks. Why don't you go anymore? By remembering all the fun things you used to do together, it would encourage you to revisit the places where you fell in love or find even better places now that your relationship has matured.

You can spend time with your spouse while you recall these great memories. Crack open the photo albums, and tell each other stories from those important days. Got any home movies? If you are married, did someone record the event? Sit down and watch it together. Make it a special event. If you can see the way you looked and felt when you first fell in love, it can make you take a step back and think about what changed. You still love your partner or spouse, and he or she still cares for you, too, and despite all the other things that have entered your life, you can feel that way again. Knowing that your spouse or partner was capable of making you feel love and passion should bring you comfort. It is possible for the two of you to feel that way again.

Looking back at how you and our partner met and fell in love will make you remember all the qualities that made your significant other stand out to you. You will want to recreate those moments that made your heart race or filled you with passion. You and your partner will want to create future love-filled memories that you will cherish later in your life.

Profess Your Love Often and in Many Ways

I know this probably seems obvious, and it goes along with the lines of being verbally affectionate, but make sure your spouse knows that you still love him or her. Sure, you may have been in a relationship for a long time, and you may even have children together, so it doesn't seem necessary to state your feelings because it's "understood." Say it, anyway; tell your spouse or partner that you love him or her multiple times a day.

Love: Fall In Love Again

Your relationship could be fading because you aren't taking the time to profess your love. This could cause your partner to become concerned that you've fallen out love with him or her because you've stopped saying it, or you don't act as you used to anymore. Whatever the reason, whether it is being too busy, tired, or otherwise, you must tell your spouse that you love him or her. It must be genuine and sincere. Say it before you leave for the day, and say it before you fall asleep at night. Say it when he or she makes you laugh. It's easy to make your partner feel happy and important, and you'll feel good about saying it, too.

Take the doubt out of things. When you first started seeing each other, you probably wanted to profess your love for all to hear, and you probably did it often. Show your spouse or partner that this side of you still exists. your partner will be surprised and will feel the desire to get back into that kind of relationship.

You can profess your love by implementing many of the suggestions that you have read and will continue to read in this book. Show your spouse or partner how much you love him or her by showering him or her with attention and taking him or her to places that are exciting and fun. Hold your partner in your arms, and tell him or her how comfortable and happy he or she makes you. Kiss your partner, and share your passions and aspirations. Put your partner or spouse first, and make him or her feel validated and important. If you are going out of your way to make your significant other feel loved and special, he or she will know without a shadow of a doubt how you feel about him or her and that you want this relationship to remain strong. Your spouse or partner will be so thrilled at the attention that he or she will also want to profess his or her love for you. Take turns, making each other feel loved. It will be a happy, healthy, and wonderful competition!

If you and your partner take the time to show each other that you love one another every day, you will feel appreciated, and your love for one another will become stronger than ever.

Take a Break

Is the tension in your relationship a relatively new problem? Look around at your demands. Are your schedules just too crazy to find time for each other? Are you both feeling stressed, and is it carrying over to your relationship or marriage? Take time out.

This could be as simple as clearing your schedules to do nothing but hang out together on the couch at home. Order take out, and watch television. Go to bed early, and just cuddle and talk. Acknowledge the fact that you both are feeling overworked and underappreciated. Taking this mental break can rejuvenate your mind and soul, but it will also help you and your partner's relationship. Practice being a good listener; be open and honest about what's troubling you, and you can start over the next day with a blank slate.

Sometimes, it can be good for you and your significant other to take time away from the chaos that is life by actually going on a vacation. It could be as short as an overnight stay or as long as you think you realistically need. You could stay as close to home or as far away as you both desire. Trips are important because you can address what's going on with your relationship, as well as spend quality time together that can make your bond stronger than ever. Turn off your phones, and try to leave the stresses of work behind. If you are both relaxed and enjoying yourselves, it will be easy to get along.

Make new memories. Even if you are going somewhere for a day or two, there are plenty of places to go and things to see. Go out to dinner, and soak up every moment of the place you are visiting and each other. Sleep until you aren't tired anymore. Make love in the middle of the day. When you can let your guard down and just worry about each other, you can love without reserve. Be reminded of who your spouse or partner is and why you love him or her. When you return home, it will be easier to keep these feelings alive.

When you return home, try to remember all of the wonderful things you did on your trip with your spouse or partner. Just like the list you made describing all your partner's best qualities, you will want to think of the time together when you find yourself becoming frustrated with your significant other. Focus on the wonderful time that you had together. Think of how happy and carefree you were while you were away from home. Think positively; you are both strong and committed to each other, and you are capable of feeling the same way even though you are home and have other things demanding your time and attention in life. There will be opportunities for you to spend time like that with your spouse or partner. If you work hard, you will be rewarded.

Another way to recall the way you felt on this vacation is to make a photo album, scrapbook, or journal entry about your experiences. Just like having mementos from the beginning of your relationship, making something from this stage of your relationship is also important because it will show you how far you've come and how you and your partner still have feelings for one another. You can look back at it when times are tough. It can then be something that motivates you to be the best partner or spouse that you can be so that you can continue to have special moments like those that you had on your vacation. Most importantly, having a record of your good times together is a testament to your relationship, and you should be proud of those memories.

Make Each Other a Priority

When you first started a relationship with your spouse or partner, you probably spent a lot of time together. It was new. You wanted to learn as much about your significant other as you could. You wanted to hold your partner's hand, experience the world with him or her, and receive attention in return. If you couldn't see each other in person, you could talk on the phone, text, or Skype. Your partner or spouse was the most important person in your world at the time. During that crucial stage of your relationship, you discovered what attracted you to your partner, and you discovered all of the reasons why you wanted him or her in your life, and by doing so, you fell in love with your significant other.

Back then, your spouse or partner was a priority. The reason why your relationship might be under stress is that other things have taken priority. Some of these might be situations beyond your control. You both could have full-time jobs that require a lot of attention. You may have children, pets, or other family members that require constant monitoring or care. However, it's also possible that you have let superficial things come between you and your spouse or partner. It could be completely harmless; maybe you love your weekly poker nights, or you work out at the gym every day for a long time. Whatever it might be, you and your partner are no longer a top priority, and that's a problem.

Love: Fall In Love Again

You have to find a way to make your significant other the number one aspect of your life. You fell in love with and committed to each other. You must continue to prove that your partner or spouse is important to you. This can be achieved easily. When you make time for your partner as well as let him or her know what he or she means to you, it will be clear to you see your partner as a priority. Sometimes, it requires compromise. While you want your spouse or partner to be happy, your wellbeing also matters. You can show your partner how important he or she is or how much you love him or her without having to give up everything in your life. You can have your poker night, but also make sure that you make yourself more available to your partner on the nights that you are home. If exercising and keeping fit is something that makes you feel whole, there's no need to give it up. Maybe cut down to fewer days, or don't stay as long as you currently do. If your significant other sees that you are attempting to make him or her a priority, he or she will want to do the same for you.

You can still be attentive to your spouse or partner without having to be negligent to other responsibilities. Taking care of your family is equally as important as your spouse or partner. However, someday, your family will grow and begin lives of their own, and when the dust settles, you still want to be in love with your significant other, right? Being a great parent is wonderful and something that you can both bond over, but at the end of the day, make sure that you still make time for each other. Be proud of who you are if you have little ones who depend on you; just don't forget where you came from. Someday, you'll be glad that you found the passion in your relationship even when it matured and changed into more than just each other.

Do you have a demanding job? Do you find it hard to disengage and not take it home with you? Remember that the best way to balance everything in life is to live in moderation. While it's important to have a career and to be the best employee that you can be, do you want to look back on your life and have regrets? Work hard, but find time to take a break. Even if it's only for a few hours a day, make that your time to be with your spouse. Talk about anything but your job. Ignore your phone and emails. It will be a stress release for you, and it will also help your spouse or partner feel validated and show him or her that he or she is the most important thing in your life. Make sure that you don't "bring work home" with you unless you absolutely have to, and if there are times that you don't have a choice but to stay late or focus on your job at home, find ways to make it up to your partner when you finally get a break. Use some of that paycheck on something fun for both of you!

As with many aspects of keeping a relationship strong, if your partner becomes a priority, you can remember why he or she is worth making compromises for. Your partner sees the effort that you are making, and it causes him or her to want to improve the relationship as well. If you are both working hard to please the other, it will be easy to fall in love again. If you are both the most important thing in each other's lives, it will be hard to find fault in each other.

Chapter Ten: Improving Communication

Couples need to communicate well because communication is the foundation of every relationship. Every relationship is emotional, and it will rely on both interpersonal nonverbal and verbal exchanges between two people. Every marriage starts with the idea that it will succeed. What couples do not worry about is communication, and what they do not know is that one of the main reasons for divorce is ineffective communication. There are three types of communication: written, nonverbal, and verbal. In this chapter, we will look at some of the most effective techniques that couples can use to improve communication.

Listen!

This is one of the most important things to do. You must listen to each other. Never talk at the same time. This is quite obvious. Many couples forget to listen. When their emotions are running high, people always want to get their point across. The idea of power comes into play here, and it goes without saying that neither wants to listen to the other. You must ensure that you do not interrupt each other. When you constantly interrupt your partner, it will come off as you not being interested in what he or she is saying. Your partner will believe that you are the only person who wants to talk. You need things to always go your way. When you are conversing with your partner, you need to hear each other out. Try to reduce the urge to interrupt your partner.

Think Before You Speak

As King Solomon said, "Give me the gift of a listening heart." If you say something mean to someone, you should understand that it could never be taken back. If you cannot speak with your partner in person, you should try to use written methods to communicate. You can text each other using short sentences. You can write your partner a note or letter. Having said that, it is best to communicate verbally. If you do choose to write notes or letters, you should not use capital letters. It is never good to write or type in caps as it gives your partner the idea that you are shouting at him or her. However, you can tell your partner that you love him or her in caps.

Show Your Partner That You Care

When you communicate with your partner, you mustn't lose sight of the fact that you are communicating to strengthen your bond. Always put yourself in your partner's shoes. Understand why your partner feels the way he or she does. Make sure you have all the facts. Do you think your partner is craving for your attention? Regardless, you need to ensure that you treat his or her feelings in the right manner. Let your partner know that his or her emotions are important. For instance, if your partner tells you that he or she is upset about not being invited to an event that he or she really wanted to attend, you need to let your partner speak. Yes, this may be silly, but you should not express your thoughts. You should instead empathize with your partner. Tell him or her that you understand that this was important to him or her, and you both will work towards understanding why he or she was not invited. This may not be possible, but your partner will love the fact that you listened. Remember that it is always the little things that count.

Do Not Hit Below the Belt

You must ensure that you watch what you say. If you resort to name-calling, you will terminate effective communication. You should also ensure that you do not bring something up from the past. If you both were in a situation where something wrong happened and you have forgiven each other, do not talk about that situation. Do not use the words "you" or "you always" in any conversation. These words will only direct the conversation negatively. Make sure that you always call your partner by his or her name or a nickname. When you do this, it will dilute the anger. This will allow you to change the tone of the conversation.

Stick to the Facts

This is one of the most important rules that you should stick to. If there is something you want to ask your partner, do so. If you are unable to find any proof, you should let the issue go. In simple words, if you do not have any proof, never bring the issue to the table. You can be suspicious, but when you accuse your partner of something, it is a different matter. Partners are often tired of being accused of having cheated. Cheaters will often claim that they have always been accused of cheating. Yes, you can be jealous, but it is not normal if you constantly express it. You can investigate very discreetly if you want to, but do not accuse your partner if you are not sure.

Be Honest and Sincere

Remember that a conversation is always between two people. Never give your partner the silent treatment. You need to know that hate, not indifference, is the opposite of love. You should always talk to your partner without any hidden intentions. You need to be honest and transparent about whatever you are saying. If you are too busy, you need to let your partner know. Then tell your partner that you will talk to each other at a different time. Never walk out of the door. You are in the relationship together.

Observe

You must understand what it is that your partner is trying to say even when he or she is not saying anything out loud. When you are in a relationship, you need to learn more about each other. Understand your partner's fears, values, dreams, and goals. Remember that you need to know your partner better than anybody else. Some people are better at expressing themselves. For example, you may know that your partner wants a new look. He or she may have gained a few pounds or have a few strands of gray hair. He or she may have become self-conscious. If you understand this, you should make sure that you support your partner.

Read Body Language

Body language will speak very loudly. This is something you need to observe. When your partner is talking to you, make sure always to look him or her in the eyes. This will show your partner that you are giving your undivided attention. When you

Love: Fall In Love Again

lean forward, it will show that you are interested in everything he or she is telling you. Make sure to understand your partner's body language better. For instance, when you observe your partner, you will see that he or she has a different way of walking for every mood. All you need to do is observe his or her walk to understand how he or she feels. When you communicate with your partner, make sure that you read his or her body language. This is the only way you can determine if you understand, disagree, or agree with him or her.

Respect Your Partner

You should never lose sight of the fact that you and your partner are a team. You cannot degrade each other only because some issues crop up. The same goes with fighting. A couple that learns to solve problems together will be successful. You cannot solve every problem together because you and your partner are individuals. You will have a different opinion in every situation. All you need to do is realize that your relationship is bigger than any issue that the two of you have. You also need to respect your partner and be a confidant. Ensure that you are someone he or she can depend on.

Third-Party Interventions

Couples also seek counseling at times. They may choose to meet a trusted family member or friend who will play a neutral role. This is never a bad idea because another person can diffuse the situation by giving you both a different perspective. You only need to ensure that the person you ask to help you has the necessary qualifications or is a confidant.

Effective communication is an important skill that every couple should have. This will help improve the marriage or relationship. This communication can be verbal, written, or nonverbal.

Steps to Improve Communication

Here are some more points to bear in mind. You know that as a couple, you need to talk and listen to each other. What most couples fail to realize is that communication is not easy. It is important to understand that communication will involve specific skills that couples need to learn and develop if they want to talk or listen to loved ones. Here are the steps that you need to master if you want to improve communication between you and your partner.

1. Approach the conversation
2. Talk to your partner
3. Listen to your partner
4. Determine the reality

Step One: Approach the Conversation

When you enter a conversation with your partner, you need to disarm unilaterally. Remember that you are not going into a war. You do not have to win. You need to give up the need always to be right. You should be willing to compromise. You can be provoked, angry, or frustrated because you have every right to feel the way you do, but you need to wait patiently and

Love: Fall In Love Again

listen to what your partner needs to say. Please do not fight back.

Step Two: Talk to Your Partner

When you enter any conversation, there is only one thing you can be sure of – your thoughts. You know how you feel about a situation and what you perceive. You do not know anything else. You do not know how your partner feels about the situation. The fact is that you may not even know what is actually happening between the two of you. All you and your partner need to bring to the conversation are your feelings, perceptions, and thoughts.

Step Three: Listen to Your Partner

As mentioned in the previous step, you do not know what your partner thinks or feels. His or her body language and other signs may give his or her emotions away. You may have exchanged some heated words in the morning, and he or she left home angry. What you do not understand is that if you do not listen to your partner, you do not know for certain about how he or she feels. Listening is a skill that you need to develop and learn. Listening is very different from hearing, and this is something that you need to understand. It is only when you listen that you know what the person is saying to you.

Step Four: Determine the Reality

When you and your partner listen to each other, you will learn more about each other. You need to listen to each other so you understand each other better. This level of understanding, along with compassion and empathy, will help to clarify the confusion between you. When you understand each other better, you can get rid of any miscommunications, misconceptions, and misinterpretations. You will finally have a clear picture of your relationship and yourself. When you listen to each other, you will understand what the issue is at any point in time and sort it out.

Chapter Eleven: Love Language

There are two forms of communication humans use to express themselves – verbal and non-verbal communication. We all speak in different languages and have different ways of expressing ourselves. Would you be able to understand someone if he or she talks to you in French and you only speak English? Maybe if you both try through gestures, you might understand what the other is saying, but it is not easy. Likewise, even love has a specific language. How do you express your love for your partner? Do you say I love you, or do you prefer to hug? These two things are quite different because they belong to different love languages.

In his book, Gary Chapman introduced the idea of love languages in 1992, "The five love languages: How to express heartfelt commitment to our mate." He believes there are five primary means through which humans express and experience love. Simply put, your love language is how you express and show your love. It also determines how you would want to receive love. To understand yourself and your partner, it is important to learn about the different love languages. Once you understand the love languages, find yours and that of your partner.

Types of Love Languages

We all have different love languages. It is not necessary for people in love to share a similar language. However, as with any other language, the good news is, you can learn to speak each other's love language. Take a moment and think about your childhood. Was there a specific way in which your parents showed their love to you? Perhaps they hugged you in the morning or gave you a good night kiss, or maybe they drove you to your favorite ice cream shop after all your games. Even if all these acts are quite different, they are all used to express their love.

Depending on your childhood and all the circumstances in your life, your love language changes. If your parents told you how much they loved you and hugged you, words of affirmation and physical touch were their love languages. If they cheered you on at all your school games and took you to places you loved, their love language was through spending quality time and acts of service. This simple example would have shown you the difference between different love languages. In this section, let us look at the five love languages.

Through Touch

When you think about a love language expressed through physical touch, sex and intimacy might be your first thoughts. However, it is so much more than just sex and physical intimacy. People whose primary love language is physical touch show their love and affection for others through physical gestures. It could be something as simple as holding your partner's hand, a warm hug, or even a massage at the end of the day. Physical affection is the only way they express their love.

Words of Love

Some people are verbally expressive about their love. It might bring to mind a scene right out of Romeo and Juliet, with the protagonists expressing and declaring their love for each other through elaborate verses and poems. Before you start worrying about your poetry skills, words of love or words of affirmation can be quite simple. It could be something as simple as saying, "I love you," or, "I miss you," to your partner. You don't need a reason to say these things, and a person whose primary language of love is words of affirmation would understand this notion. Such people express their love and affection for others through their appreciation, praise, and the words they speak.

Acts of Love

For an individual whose primary love language is acts of love, making any gestures or performing different tangible tasks for his or her loved one is the means of communicating love. For instance, cooking a meal for your loved one or cleaning the car could be your way of expressing your love.

Spending Time Together

As the name suggests, spending quality time together is also a love language. This is so much more than just sitting together and watching mindless television. It's about spending uninterrupted, one-on-one, and intimate time with your loved ones. Involving in real and honest conversations and meaningful interactions is a part of this love language.

Giving Gifts

We all love gifts. Who wouldn't want to be spoiled with gifts? Well, this is precisely what an individual with this love language believes. An individual whose primary love language is receiving gifts would express his or her love for others by giving meaningful and thoughtful presents. It's not about making grand gestures but about giving gifts that others would enjoy.

Importance of Love Language

Our expression of love and how we feel are quite different. By understanding these differences, it becomes easier for a couple to stay on the same page. An effortless way to improve and strengthen your relationship is by understanding each other's love language. If your means of expressing your love is quite different from that of your partner, you both might run into trouble if you do not realize this difference. You might both be in love with each other, but the inability to understand your partner's love language can cause communication difficulties and misunderstandings. Your way of saying I love you is to cook your partner's favorite meals, whereas he or she might express love by giving you thoughtful gifts. If you don't reciprocate your partner's love language, he or she might believe the love isn't mutual. This line of thought applies to you, too. By understanding and learning each other's love language, you can strengthen your bond.

According to "Speaking the language of relational maintenance: A validity test of Chapman's (1992) five love languages" (2006), the five love languages offer an effective framework for a couple to communicate with each other. Apart from better communication, here are some more benefits of understanding each other's love language in a relationship.

Meaningful Actions

When a couple finally understands each other's love language and starts speaking in the same language, every act becomes more meaningful; when your acts become more intentional and meaningful, the love increases. When you say, "I love you," in a way that makes more sense to your partner, the interaction automatically becomes more meaningful. In turn, it would make your partner feel more loved, cherished, understood, appreciated, and happy. If your partner reciprocates all this, it will strengthen the relationship and create space for more happiness.

More Empathy

When you learn about you and your partner's expression and experience love, your ability to empathize increases, empathy is known as the ability to experience and understand what the other person feels as if the emotion is your own. Simply put, it is one's ability to step into the other person's shoes. When you communicate in your partner's love language, you are essentially stepping out of your own perspective and are looking at the situation from your partner's view. By doing things that are meaningful to your partner, you can make the other person feel loved and significant.

If you and your partner commit yourself to learning each other's love language, your shared emotional intelligence increases. It helps you place someone else's needs before your own. Instead of speaking in the language you understand, it prompts you to speak in a language your partner understands. After all, a message isn't fully communicated until the other person understands.

Personal Growth and Development

Let us take the point as mentioned earlier a step further. When you finally think from someone else's perspective and place his or her needs above your own, it enhances your personal growth. The current society we live in promotes a culture based on self-absorption and selfishness. We are preoccupied with our own needs, wants, and desires that we barely have any time to concentrate on someone else.

By learning, understanding, and communicating in your partner's love language, you are finally concentrating on someone other than yourself. It essentially forces you to step outside your comfort zone. If you learn to do this, it creates more opportunities for growth and development. After all, change occurs outside your comfort zone.

Better Intimacy

By finally communicating in each other's love language, it becomes easier to maintain and increase intimacy in any relationship. When you learn about each other and discover new ways to communicate with each other on a deeper level, intimacy will increase. If you realize your partner's primary love language is physical touch, you can start adding more physical gestures to your love language.

Selflessness

When you combine all the points mentioned until now, you will realize concentrating on someone else's love language increases your selfishness. Instead of convincing or forcing your partner to learn your love language, take a moment to learn his or her own. By doing this, you are essentially prioritizing your partner's needs above your own. This is also the central idea upon which Dr. Chapman's theory of love languages is based on. In an ideal scenario, the partners in a relationship would want to express love in a meaningful way. However, the idea of learning love language is to express your love for your partner in a way that he or she understands.

Decoding the Love Language

Now that you are aware of the five love languages, it is important to identify yours and your partner's. Once you have identified all this, learn to show your partner how much you love him or her in his or her language. Are you wondering how you can do this? Well, here are some simple tips that you can use.

Through Touch

If your partner's love language is based on physical touch, try to express your love physically. From holding hands to random hugs and pats on the back, there are different things you can use to express your love. Touch your partner's hand during a conversation, hug him or her before heading out in the morning, or offer a massage at the end of a tiring day. You can cuddle with your partner while watching TV, hold hands whenever you go for a walk, or gently put your arm around him or her while out for a meal. The more physically expressive you are about your love, the more understood and appreciated your partner would feel.

Words of Love

Any individual whose love language is based on affirmation would not only want but also need to hear the words "I love you." If your partner falls in this category, ensure that you express your love through words. It could be a love note, a voice message, or even a conversation where you tell your partner about the different things you love about him or her. If your partner cooks a delicious meal of you, don't forget to thank him or her; words of affirmation could be in the form of praise, encouragement, compliments, or reminders of his or her true potential. If your partner hits a weight loss goal, don't forget to congratulate him or her. Compliment your partner about his or her dressing style, hair, or even cooking. There are different things you can do to express your love verbally, and try to do it more often.

Acts of Love

If your partner's primary love language is based on acts of love and service, any gesture or service you do that eases your partner's burden and responsibility would be appreciated. If you are running out of ideas, you can always ask your partner what he or she would like you to do to make his or her life easier. Simple acts of service could be getting your partner's car washed, vacuuming the house once in a while, cooking his or her favorite meal, or even offering to do the dishes. The acts don't have to be anything grand and significant. Even simple acts will be well appreciated. The only thing that matters is you understand your partner's love language and try to communicate in it.

Spending Time Together

If your partner's primary love language is based on spending quality time together, the simplest thing is to spend more time together. By spending time together, it doesn't mean sitting quietly in a room. Instead, it's about indulging in meaningful conversations and spending one-on-one time. While doing this, get rid of all your distractions. Even if it's only 20 minutes at the end of the day, ensure all your attention is dedicated to your partner. These 20 minutes would mean more than any lavish gift you could give. Maintain eye contact while having a conversation, plan specific date nights, create romantic events, or simply catch up for a coffee after work. During this period, all your partner requires is your undivided attention.

Giving Gifts

If your partner's love language falls under this category, any effort and thought that goes into the gift gives matters more than the gift itself. Such individuals not only love receiving gifts but also love giving gifts. This is the only way in which they know how to express that love. When it comes to such partners, by giving them the right gift, you are essentially expressing your love. It also shows you understand your partner's love language. The gift doesn't have to be elaborate, expensive, or grand. Instead, it needs to be thoughtful and heartfelt. For instance, it could be something as simple as getting your partner's favorite candy or making a trinket. Also, there are bonus points for every major occasion you remember and get him or her a gift for.

Chapter Twelve: Healing Negative Cycles in a Relationship

Learning to identify, understand, and fix negative relationship patterns is essential for a long-term relationship. Two of the most important foundations on which all healthy and lasting relationships rest are intimacy and respect. Intimacy and respect provide a sense of freedom, connection, and security. Without these things, there can be no trust in a relationship. Once the trust is lost, the partners' ability to be happy, spontaneous, or even accommodating diminishes drastically.

In this chapter, we'll look at some of the most common issues that can damage the love and happiness in any relationship if left unchecked. You will learn to identify these issues and fix or overcome them. Once you pay attention to these patterns, understand how the problem cropped up, and are willing to put in the effort required to heal your relationship, overcoming these issues becomes easier.

Issue #1: The Blame Game

We all like to take credit for all the good in our lives. However, when it comes to mistakes and plans going awry, we often point fingers. It's quite easy to shift the blame on to someone else and shrug away all responsibility for a bad outcome. At times, we might also attribute such unfavorable outcomes to our partners. If you knowingly or unknowingly believe you have a better way of doing things, know better than your partner, or constantly try to fix your partner, things will take a turn for the worse.

Remember, you are not a puppeteer, and your partner is not perfect. Do not look at your partner like he or she is a project you need to tinker with or fine-tune. Instead, you need to understand that your partner is your equal in the relationship, and it's never about perfection. After all, we are all humans, and perfection is merely a mirage.

If blaming and fixing are undesirable, why do a lot of people indulge in such behaviors? The problem is our brain constantly looks for different reasons to justify the outcomes. While it does this, it is also trying to fix the problem. Our ancestors probably had better chances of survival because of this coping mechanism. These days, we don't need similar survival instincts because modern life is quite different. As the brain is incapable of differentiating between an actual and real threat with an apparent threat, such as stress, its response to both these situations is the same. In a bid to protect itself, the brain actively looks for causes when something goes wrong and tries to fix it. Some love to control everything in their life, and their romantic relationships and partners are no exception. Such individuals feel unsafe if they don't exert their control over others. The simplest way to have more control over the outcome is to blame and try to fix one's partner.

There is seldom a single facet to every problem, and correctly identifying it isn't always possible. For instance, a highly educated and talented individual might not find a job that's on par with the skills he or she offers because of the geographical location or poor financial conditions of the economy. Likewise, at times, when things go wrong, it isn't always a single partner's fault.

Certain basic traits, such as emotional sensitivity, intelligence, energy levels, or introversion, cannot be changed. While viewing a situation, your perspective matters a lot. These characteristics and traits often play a major role in influencing your perception of the events that transpired. Remember that no two individuals are alike, and therefore, our perceptions and perspective of the situation also change. You might be viewing the issue from a specific perspective while your partner has a different perspective. Unknowingly, you might be viewing the situation through your own biases and distortions, which, in turn, prompts you to shift the blame.

Another reason why blaming and fixing are problematic is because they increase the risk of miscommunication and other negative cycles based on hurt, anger, or grief. When you constantly blame someone else, it's quite likely, after a point, that the other person stops listening and responding. After all, who will be fine with being blamed for every little thing?

When you start blaming someone, you are essentially conveying that he or she is at fault while you are right. In an attempt to prove yourself right in all situations, you might be compromising on the basic pillars of a relationship. After a while, the need to always be right might surpass the primary psychological needs satisfied by a relationship, such as safety, connection, or even influence. For instance, let's assume you and your partner had an unpleasant discussion. The discussion was getting heated, and you were trying to prove your partner was acting poorly, and vice versa. If you both keep doing this, the discussion will only worsen and lead to arguments and fights. There is no room to resolve an issue when fingers are being pointed and the blame game is going on.

The good news is all this can be easily circumvented. Before you start assuming someone else made a mistake, it's important to take a long, hard look at your actions. It's quite easy to point fingers at others, but remember, we all make mistakes, and we are all flawed. Also, work on assuming that your partner might have unintentionally or unwittingly contributed to a specific problem. Learn to take responsibility for your own mistakes, problems, and actions. If you believe your partner's actions have truly hurt you, start talking about it. Whenever you have such discussions, use "I" sentences. For instance, if you feel your partner is unsupportive or extremely critical of you, don't say, "You never support me," or, "Why can't you be more like ___?" Instead, talk about your feelings and needs – those that were not met – instead of harping on what your partner should have done. You could say something like, "I feel unsupported when you don't actively listen to what I say."

Issue #2: Emotional Distancing

Emotional intimacy is as important as physical intimacy in a relationship. If you and your partner don't share an emotional connection, the relationship is bound to wither away sooner or later. It's essential for couples to openly and honestly communicate about different feelings and emotions that are important to them. If the primary emotions are not dealt with effectively, they can manifest themselves as undesirable secondary emotions, such as anger. For instance, if you feel your partner doesn't pay any attention to you, instead of talking about the unfulfilled need, resorting to passive-aggressive behavior to gain attention creates a negative relationship cycle. A lot of people tend to resort to such behavior because it helps prevent them from feeling vulnerable. Pushing your emotions aside is never a solution. It might temporarily mask the symptoms, but it doesn't treat the issue at hand.

As mentioned, people use emotional distancing as a tool to shield their vulnerabilities. Instead of talking about our deepest needs and feelings with partners, we shove these feelings away.

Emotional distancing can occur when a partner doesn't understand how to deal with the unhappiness communicated by the other. Instead of listening to the problem empathetically, their responses would be more concentrated on trying to fix the problem or defending their position. The inability to cope with difficult emotions, regardless of whether they are your own or your partner's, can result in emotional distancing.

Also, individuals who had a tough childhood, experienced loss of a loved one, or have any other unresolved issues might be afraid of dealing with their own emotions. This becomes problematic because instead of leading their lives as a unit, emotional distancing makes partners turn into two people who live together for logistical reasons.

Marriage is not a transaction or a living arrangement. Emotional distancing is bad for a marriage because it can slowly erode sexual intimacy, too. Once the sexual flames die, emotional distance increases. If partners are unable to talk to each other, the marriage turns into a roommate agreement. When the feelings of loneliness and hurt are left unaddressed, they could manifest in different ways. One or both the partners might start concentrating more than necessary on their work or social status or might even have affairs to compensate for all their unmet needs. This, in turn, makes both the partners lead their own individual lives. Simply put, emotional distancing could break any relationship.

Are you wondering how this problem can be rectified? As with most of the other problems in our lives, communication is important in a relationship. Please go through the different tips about communication discussed in this book, and start implementing them today. Be honest and authentic about your needs, not just with yourself but with your partner, too. Start talking about all these things without any hesitation, apprehension, and fear. If you cannot communicate honestly with each other, there is no point in the relationship. Be willing to change, and listen to your partner with an open mind. By merely listening to your partner, you can understand the problem at hand.

If you believe it is needed, seek therapy proactively. At times, couple's counseling is a great way to heal any emotional distance in the relationship. If couple's therapy is not required, the individual partners could concentrate on their insecurities, fears, and unresolved issues to deal with the relationship's negative cycles.

Another way to restore emotional intimacy in a relationship is by working on sexual intimacy. When you physically connect with the other person, it becomes easier to strike an emotional chord. You will discover more practical tips to do all these things in the subsequent chapters.

Issue #3: Trust Fades Away

A happy, healthy, and lasting relationship is based on mutual trust and understanding. The inability to trust your partner can manifest itself in different forms. You might start believing your partner is hiding something from you or is dishonest or unreliable. If you don't trust your partner, you might believe he or she wouldn't be there for you. You might also start from believing he or she is in the relationship to take advantage of you. If you don't trust your partner, staying in the relationship can become unbearable. It could also manifest itself in the form of several insecurities. Without trust, neither of you can be honest and open about your desires, wants, or needs.

Love: Fall In Love Again

When it comes to marriage, there is always a reason why two individuals decide to spend their life together. More than concentrating on common values, we often find a partner who possesses a specific skill, trait, or characteristic that we lack. No two individuals are alike, and you can never find someone who would agree with everything you say. With time, our needs, wants, and desires change. Once this happens, the initial charm of the relationship slowly fades away. When this charm goes away, the partners' willingness to put up with each other's differences decrease.

Another reason for the lack of trust could be personal insecurities, such as jealousy or the fear of abandonment. If you keep trying to control your partner because you are worried he or she would find someone better, it can create trust issues. If you have a history of toxic relationships, these personal insecurities can have a stronghold over you. All these issues, when left unresolved, create a negative communication cycle that starts to eliminate trust.

In a healthy, happy, and loving relationship, the partners always support each other. There is mutual trust in the relationship, which enables both partners to grow and explore the world. When you know you are unconditionally loved and supported, it gives you immense strength that provides the courage to explore your interests and passions. The absence of trust has the opposite effect on a relationship. It tends to shrink your world and worsens any insecurity you might harbor. When there is no trust in the relationship, you automatically tend to distance yourself from your partner or alienate others. It becomes a self-fulfilling prophecy without a happy ending. Lack of trust can prompt you to push others away inadvertently and prevent you from receiving and giving genuine love.

Rather than go through all this, you can learn to fix this negative cycle by dealing with trust issues. If you realize that you or your partner has some trust issues, it's always better to address it and tackle it head-on. It is not something to sleep on, and certainly don't avoid talking about the elephant in the room. Before you concentrate on mutual trust, it's always better to look at your own issues. Can you trust yourself? If your answer is "no," it's time to address the issues you might have. Any unhealed emotional trauma, insecurities, addictions, or even depression could result in a lack of trust.

The next step is to address any issues or behaviors your partner might have indulged in that eroded your trust in the relationship. Even while you talk about these issues, ensure you don't point fingers at each other and indulge in blame. Please don't waste your time doing all these things because it merely worsens the relationship's negative pattern. Instead, talk about the issue like mature adults. Don't suppress any important aspects of your life merely to accommodate your partner. Work together as a couple, and find a solution that helps rebuild the trust in the relationship. Rebuilding trust is seldom easy, but with time, effort, and patience, it certainly can be achieved.

Issue #4: The Harsh Critic

Criticism can either be healthy or unhealthy, depending on how it is delivered. Excessive criticism and putdowns, when directed towards your partner, can effectively kill any love you feel. Any negative comments made about the other person's character, competence, physical appearance, or even desirability could be constituted as criticism. Any putdown, such as name calling or disrespectful forms of communication, will also have the same effect.

Love: Fall In Love Again

Before you learn to fix this issue, it's important to understand why people often criticize others or put them down. There are different reasons why people criticize their loved ones. A simple reason is emotional upbringing or childhood. If you saw your family members relate to each other by resorting to criticism and putdowns, you might believe it is okay to dole out the same treatment to your partner. Another reason could be a psychological factor, such as narcissism. For instance, narcissists are scared of intimacy and are often on guard, looking for flaws in their partners. Their fear of intimacy makes them a faultfinding machine. The moment they notice an apparent or perceived flaw in their partner, they use it as an indication of their poor judgment.

Apart from this, repressed emotions, especially anger, could manifest itself in barbed comments and harsh criticism. Any unaddressed problems or fears associated with the relationship, when left unregulated, will eventually find their way to the surface. People resort to criticism and putdowns because they are untrusting of others or have a primary fear of abandonment. They use barbed comments to control their partners.

Why is it bad to be a harsh critic? At times, it is okay to correct your partner when he or she is wrong or make a mistake. However, if all you do is constantly criticize your partner, it will erode his or her self-confidence and take away the trust in the relationship. Remember that we are all human, and nobody is perfect. We all have our weaknesses and flaws. A strong relationship is based on unconditional love and acceptance. It is quite easy to love something that perfect. True love is based on your ability to accept the other person despite his or her flaws. When love becomes conditional, it makes the relationship a living nightmare.

If you are stuck with someone who constantly criticizes every move you make, you would likely start questioning yourself in the end. A simple consequence of this could be the end of any relationship. If you don't want to end your relationship, it's time to fix such negative patterns. Are you wondering how you can fix it? The answer is quite simple. Learn to be compassionate and tolerant of your partner. You cannot turn your partner into a flawless being, and the sooner you accept it, the better it is for your relationship. If there are things you don't like about your partner, instead of being harsh, think about the reasons that prompted your partner to act the way he or she did. Instead of trying to fix your partner, it's better to work on any issues you feel are left unaddressed.

If your partner makes a mistake, you can talk to him or her about it with love and compassion instead of doling out harsh criticism. This rule not only applies to you but to your partner, too. If you are quick to pounce on each other's mistakes, the relationship will quickly turn into a battleground. For instance, if your partner doesn't do the dishes, instead of saying, "You never do anything around the house, and I'm tired of it," you can say, "I am quite tired and stressed out today. It would be wonderful if you could help me with the dishes." The message you are conveying is the same in both these scenarios, and the only difference is how it was conveyed.

Chapter Thirteen: Deal with Arguments

Spats are quite common when two people live together. Married couples argue and have certain disputes. All these things are not only normal but are to be expected in a marriage. However, the real trouble starts when the couple doesn't know how to deal with the spats. If left unregulated, a simple spat can easily spin out of control and compromise the integrity of the marriage itself.

The health of your relationship, especially in the long run, is determined by your ability to handle and positively deal with any squabbles. The ability to overcome a squabble and get back to your partner with compassion, unconditional love, and support is one of the most excellent perks of a healthy and strong relationship. If the very foundation of your relationship starts shaking at the slightest sign of trouble, it isn't good news. From arguing about finances to the frequency of sex, children, or even what to have for a meal, there are different things that couples argue about. These arguments can cause a lot of emotional stress and result in insecurity.

Even if there are different things that couples fight about, there seems to be a common point in all of these fights. The inability of a couple to compromise or reach a mutually agreeable solution in case of a difference in opinions or values results in fights. In any relationship where one partner has extremely high expectations and isn't willing to compromise or accommodate, the frequency of fights will be high.

There are two common mistakes that couples make when dealing with arguments or unpleasant conversations. The first mistake is that they don't give each other a fair chance to communicate about the different things they have on their minds. After all, the only way to sort out a problem or deal with an issue is by talking about it. If you or your partner is not listening to the other or does not want to listen, communication becomes exceedingly difficult.

The second common mistake is an unwillingness to accept responsibility for one's role in the argument. After all, an argument is a heated discussion. A discussion involves two people. If the partners do not accept their mistakes, they become unwilling to apologize and keep defending their position. Instead of fixing the issue, the argument will spiral out of control. When these little arguments are put together, it increases the emotional strain on the relationship in the long run. This results in feelings of resentment, annoyance, deep-seated anger, or even frustration, and there are different ways in which these repressed emotions come to the surface.

Think of all the unaddressed issues in a relationship as the pressure building up in a pressure cooker. What happens after a while? If this pressure isn't let out, eventually, the cooker bursts. This is precisely what happens to marriages when partners are unwilling to resolve any of the deep-seated issues. However, there is some good news. Learning to deal with arguments constructively and positively is possible. In this chapter, you learn about some simple tips you can use to deal with an argument, resolve conflict, and prevent it from worsening.

Take a Break

Whenever you discuss something with your partner and believe your emotions are flaring up, it's time to break from the conversation. It doesn't mean you walk away from the conversation or physically distance yourself from it. Instead, it merely means you are required to stay silent until you feel calm. It's quite easy to say harsh things when you lose your temper. By choosing silence first, you are giving yourself the time required to calm down so you can rationally think about the situation. This is also a great way to regain control of your emotions. When emotions are running high, rationality goes out of the window. Even if you stay silent for a couple of seconds, it gives you a chance to look at the situation from your partner's perspective. Instead of defending your position, you can find some common ground without perpetuating the unpleasant situation.

Understand Limits

Before you ask your partner for something, remember that if the roles were reversed, you should be willing to do what you are about to ask your partner. So, never ask your partner for anything that you wouldn't be willing to do yourself. Regardless of what it is that you are asking, ensure it is something you can do. For instance, you might ask your partner to stay calm or start saving for an exotic vacation. Ensure that you can use your behavior as an example to convey your point. If you cannot do these two things, it doesn't make any sense to ask your partner for the same.

Find Some Balance

Instead of dwelling on any negative emotions, it's always better to question them. Ask yourself why you're feeling the specific emotion. After this, think about any different situations in your past when you experienced the same emotion. Now, think of different situations in your past where you acted the way your partner is acting right now. For instance, if you are upset because your partner didn't clean the dishes, ask yourself whether this is the only reason why you are upset. Once you answer this, it's time to consider whether you have indulged in similar behavior in the past. If you have, then maybe your anger isn't warranted in this situation.

It is quite easy to find fault with someone else while ignoring your own faults. This is a common mistake a lot of couples make. Instead of nitpicking on the flaws or mistakes your partner has while ignoring your flaws, it would be better to work on solutions. Focusing on your partner's mistakes causes a lot of imbalance in the relationship and increases unpleasant conversations and unresolved issues. In fact, in the previous example, if you keep blaming your partner or argue with him or her for not doing the dishes, a time will come when your partner would erupt in anger.

Try Meditation

A simple way to gain some clarity is by meditating. You don't have to meditate for hours on end. Even meditating for as little as 15 minutes daily can help give you better control of your emotions and thoughts. Instead of avoiding unpleasant emotions and thoughts, meditation gives you the courage and strength required to deal with these issues head-on.

Meditation also teaches you to keep your calm. Even when your emotions are running high, when all the unpleasant emotions are reduced, it becomes easier to stay calm and think about the situation rationally. When you think rationally, the chances of fights also reduce.

Learn to Apologize

If you have done something well, you would expect praise for it, wouldn't you? Likewise, if you make a mistake or do something wrong, you need to apologize for it. Learning to take responsibility for your actions and behaviors is quite important. It also becomes easier for your partner to forgive and move on when you accept responsibility for your mistakes.

It is quite easy to reduce any emotional toxicity in the relationship by apologizing. While apologizing, ensure that it is a heartfelt and genuine apology. After apologizing, make amends, and don't repeat the same mistakes. If you keep making the same mistakes repeatedly and apologize for them, too, it becomes redundant.

Accept responsibility, apologize, and make amends. While apologizing, ensure you clearly state the reason why. You can also add how you plan to avoid similar situations in the future.

Start Forgiving

Unless you learn to forgive, it isn't easy to move on in life. If every little argument or fight you had with your partner is still weighing heavily on your mind, it's highly unlikely that you can concentrate on the present or dream about a happy future. If you and your partner are carrying a lot of emotional baggage and several unresolved issues, the next time an argument starts, most of this baggage might manifest itself in the form of ugly emotions.

Instead of all this, it would be better if a couple learns to make allowances for human behavior. After all, we are all humans, and none of us is perfect. We can aim for perfection, but we are flawed. Learning to accept your flaws and those of your partner makes it easier to deal with any situation that comes along. When you realize humans make mistakes, it becomes easier to forgive. When you forgive, you don't carry any unresolved matters with you. In turn, it gives you the clarity required to deal with an issue without combining it with any other unresolved problems or emotions you might have.

Is It a Real Problem?

Losing a loved one or being diagnosed with a life-threatening illness can be a real problem. Anything that doesn't mortally harm you or your partner isn't a real problem. Keep this simple point in mind whenever you argue with your partner. Every issue can be dealt with calmly and rationally when you learn to distinguish between a real and imaginary problem. If your partner forgets to message you because he or she was busy with work, it isn't a reason to start an argument. By asking yourself, "Is this a real problem?", you can easily gain perspective.

Love: Fall In Love Again

Remember that whenever you hit a rough patch, all you need to do is adapt and overcome whatever problem you are faced with. You shouldn't focus on the small issues; just ignore them. When you live long enough with a person, you will realize it isn't worth sweating the small stuff. Before you make a big deal out of a small issue, ask yourself if the issue in question would matter 10 years later. If you think it will not, don't fight over it.

Sofia Price

Chapter Fourteen: Offer Sympathy Not Solutions

Here is a hypothetical situation. Adam and Eve have been married for five years. Eve comes home from work in the evening and finds Adam in a bad mood. He seems frustrated, angry, upset, and disheartened. He looks like he wants to be comforted. She asks him, "Honey, what happened?" Adam starts talking about the rough day he had at work. He was passed over for a promotion he deserved because the boss was biased towards another coworker. Now, Eve tells him, "Maybe you should have worked harder. Stop feeling bad and concentrate on better things." This seems to trigger Adam, and the conversation soon turns into an argument. Adam is visibly upset now, even more than he was.

What do you think happened in this situation? The answer is quite simple – Eve offered unsolicited advice. Adam did not ask for it, and all he needed was someone to comfort him. He is aware of the things he needs to do, and the sentence, "Snap out of it, and do something better," made it seem as if Eve was dismissive of his feelings. The advice she gave wasn't wrong and was practical. However, it wasn't something that Adam needed at the time. He was looking to be comforted, and the tough love he was shown didn't work. This discussion could have waited for a while longer.

Do you and your partner have similar situations? Regardless of how well-meaning your advice is, it doesn't serve any purpose if the other person doesn't want it. When you see your loved one in trouble, it is an instinct to offer solutions to his or her problem. At times, the only thing your partner is looking for is a shoulder to lean on. Offering advice at the wrong time can be quite problematic. In this section, you will learn about the damage caused by unsolicited advice and what you can do instead.

Don't Offer Solutions

If your partner tells you about a problem or conflict they are having, what is your first impulse? Your first impulse is probably to try and fix this problem for your partner. You might offer advice and solutions. In fact, you might also believe finding the solution is the best way to fix the situation. Before you do this, ask yourself,

- Did he or she ask me for my advice?
- Does he or she need my advice?
- Why is he or she sharing this with me?

Once you answer these questions for yourself and do it honestly, you will realize that your partner probably needs someone to talk to. Before you think about empowering your partner with a solution to his or her problem, try to determine whether he or she needs your help. Usually, people look for a listening ear. Your partner is probably sharing his or her problems with you because he or she wants you to review all the options available. Your partner is seeking your sympathy and validation instead of solutions. He or she probably doesn't have anyone else to talk to about this, and your partner needs to understand whether he or she is thinking in the right direction. It might be frustrating when your partner shares his or her problems with you but doesn't want your advice. However, no one likes unsolicited

Love: Fall In Love Again

advice. No matter how well-meaning your intentions are, your partner didn't ask you for a solution. You might have a hundred and one ideas about how your partner can solve the problem. Meanwhile, it would be good to hold your tongue until he or she asks you for solutions.

Are you still wondering why you shouldn't offer solutions? Keeping your intentions aside, unsolicited advice often looks like criticism instead of helpful action. It can even make you seem judgmental and defensive of the things your partner is telling you. For instance, if your partner is sharing his or her work troubles with you and you start offering solutions immediately, it indirectly conveys a message that your partner is incompetent and that you are better equipped to deal with his or her problems. If you don't want to create unnecessary drama and instead want to deal with situations maturely. So, place yourself in your partner's shoes for a moment. Once you learn to look at the situation from your partner's perspective, you will understand what he or she needs under a given circumstance.

Unsolicited advice can also make you seem like a know-it-all or a narcissist. If your partner is sharing his or her problems with you, the first step is to listen. If you have to listen, then you need to be present at the moment. Stop thinking about the different solutions you can offer and merely concentrate on your partner's words. By listening and being there, you are doing more than you think you are.

Using sentences like these will make you seem inconsiderate and even selfish to a certain extent"

"It could be worse…"

"I think you should…"

"I believe this can be turned into a positive experience..."

"I don't think it is as big a deal as you are making it out to be..."

In fact, such statements will prevent your partner from sharing his or her troubles with you. After all, would you go to someone for comfort if he or she isn't willing to comfort you? These responses invalidate the other person's problems, as well as his or her thoughts, opinions, and feelings. It can also make your partner feel incompetent, foolish, and silly. If someone is already miserable or distraught, the addition of these feelings worsens the situation.

Offering Sympathy Works

Let's assume you had a long and tiring yet unproductive day at work. You come home feeling dejected. Now, what would you want your partner to do? You probably want your partner to comfort you, tell you it is okay, or just hug you. If you don't get these things, it merely increases the disappointment you feel. You were looking for a shoulder to lean on or a listening ear. When you were denied both these things and were offered something you didn't want, it creates frustration and resentment.

The next time such a situation occurs, remind yourself that every conversation isn't about offering solutions. Your partner is looking for your support in such instances. Your partner needs you to be present and not heap on advice that he or she didn't ask for. Here are some simple tips that will come in handy during such situations.

Role Reversal

You cannot truly be sympathetic unless you understand what the other person is saying and where he or she is coming from. For a moment, stop thinking from your perspective, and try to place yourself in your partner's shoes. What would you want, expect, or need if the roles were reversed? Ask yourself this question before you do anything else while your partner is talking to you. It broadens your perspective of the situation, gives you more insight into what the other person is feeling, and makes you more empathetic. If your partner knows he or she can count on you in times of need, then he or she will be more inclined to share his or her perspectives with you. On the other hand, if your partner knows you will not listen, he or she wouldn't want to share. After all, who would want to share when they are not heard?

Active Listening

Did you know there's a difference between hearing and listening? Yes, the words are often used synonymously, but their meaning differs. When you listen to someone, you are not only understanding the words being said but are also trying to understand where the person is coming from. Listening is a conscious process, and you need to concentrate on what someone is saying while allowing your brain to process what the sentences mean. On the other hand, when you hear someone, you are merely using your ears to perceive what is being said. Hearing is the act of collecting data, whereas listening means you pay thoughtful attention to what is being said and give it due consideration. Also, when you truly listen to what your partner says, you do not merely hear the words to process a reply but also understand the meaning behind those words.

Another aspect of active listening that you need to concentrate on is asking questions. You don't need to come up with brilliant questions. In fact, you can merely rephrase what your partner said. For instance, if your partner says he or she is upset that he or she was passed over for a promotion that he or she deserved, you could respond with, "Why is your boss biased?" When you rephrase statements into questions, it shows you are listening. The act of listening in itself is a form of validation because it also shows you are interested in what your partner is saying.

No Judgments

It is not just about actively listening to what your partner says, but you should also withhold judgment. You cannot be sympathetic to someone if you have any preconceived notions about what he or she is saying. Any bias you have will cloud your judgment and prevent you from being there for your partner. If you are already biased to what your partner says, it's quite likely you wouldn't want to listen to what he or she is saying. If you start taking responsibility for what your partner is feeling or take everything personally, it results in unnecessary blame and guilt. This merely worsens the situation. Remember, your partner is sharing his or her experiences with you and is not blaming you in any way. Concentrate only on your partner's message and nothing else. Keep an open mind, and try to be curious about what your partner is saying and why he or she feels this way.

What Your Partner Needs

Learn to be present whenever your partner needs you. If you are not there for your partner in such instances, it slowly chips away on the trust relationship. Your partner might also start believing that he or she cannot depend or count on you. If you want to be present, you need to learn to live in the moment. Forget about everything else when your partner is talking. Allow your partner to pour his or her heart out without any interruptions. If you are doubtful about what your partner needs, you could ask, "I understand what you are saying; how can I make it better for you?" or, "I understand you had a rough day; what would you want to do now?" These simple questions are so much better than unsolicited advice. Instead of telling your partner to get over it, try to put yourself in his or her shoes, and think about it from his or her perspective. This display of meaningful consideration for your partner's needs and wants makes you look more approachable and empathetic.

Offer Validation

Offering validation doesn't mean you are giving up your opinions or perspective. When you offer validation, the other person feels heard and understood. True validation comes only when you listen to what your partner is saying. Many people wrongly believe that validating someone else's feelings or perspective means they are abandoning their own. No, this is nothing more than a misconception. Offering validation is also a great way of showing empathy in a relationship.

Instead of fixing your partner or his or her problems, just be there for your partner. Even a simple "I love you, and I understand what you are going through" helps more than any advice you offer.

Chapter Fifteen: HEAL Technique

According to the statistics collected by the Centers for Disease Control and Prevention, the divorce rate was around 2.9% per 1000 of the population in 2018. Well, 2.9% doesn't sound so bad, does it? When you look at these figures from a broader perspective, it results in about 782,038 divorces in 2018 alone. These statistics are certainly quite scary. Oh boy, that's a lot of broken hearts! The good news is you have the power to prevent your marriage from ending up as one of these statistics. There are a lot of things in life that are certainly beyond your control. However, the one thing you can always control is how you respond to situations. Instead of reacting, if you learn to respond calmly to a situation, everything becomes manageable. Here is a simple example to give you a better understanding of the concept of reaction and response.

What will happen if you touch a hot plate? You will automatically drop it. Touching the hot plate is the action while dropping it without any conscious thought is the reaction. Reactions are quick, automatic, not based on any conscious thought, and can be aggressive, too. On the other hand, a response is calm, composed, thoughtful, and non-aggressive.

During an argument, it is quite easy to react harshly. We often say things in the heat of the moment. Let us assume you and your partner are in the midst of a heated argument. When you resort to exchanging insults, name-calling, or even physical violence, these actions can be termed as reactions. A response would be when you listen to each other calmly, don't let the situation escalate, and discuss the problem at hand without letting each other's emotions get out of hand.

If there were any instances when you wished you responded instead of reacted, there is no time like the present to work to improve on yourself. As a rule of thumb, make it a point for you and your partner to try to respond to situations instead of giving in to thoughtless reactions, which are often damaging. Are you wondering how you can do this? In this chapter, you will learn about a simple concept known as the HEAL technique.

HEAL is an acronym for Hear, Empathize, Act, and Love. Using this technique, you can easily replace any defensive reactions with positive responses that stem from a place of love. If you and your partner decide to follow this technique, healing negative relationship cycles, unnecessary arguments can be reduced. Are you curious to learn more about this brilliant technique?

Step One: Hear

You must learn to be present and be willing to listen to what your partner says to use the HEAL technique. Unless you do both these things, you cannot fully understand what the other person is saying. If you keep formulating your comeback while your partner talks, it increases the negativity in the relationship. Such an attitude also makes the other person feel unheard. Learn to listen to what your partner says while keeping an open heart and mind. It means you need to lower your defenses, and stop treating every argument as a battle to be won. Remember that if someone is upset about a specific issue, it is because the issue might have caused some hurt. If you hear the other person out, it becomes easier to learn and fulfill each other's desires without misunderstandings.

While listening to your partner, it is not just the words you should pay attention to. Don't just focus on the verbal aspects of communication, but concentrate on nonverbal communication as well. Usually, most of our communication is nonverbal. So, pay attention to body language, facial expressions, gestures, and eye contact. Maintain positive nonverbal communication.

While your partner is talking to you, please pay attention to his or her facial expressions. Does your partner look sad? Is there any anger or sadness in his or her eyes? Does your partner's body language look defensive? Likewise, ensure that your body language is open and doesn't come across as defensive. For instance, cross your arms while communicating shows you are defensive and are unwilling to listen to what others say. Try to understand what your partner might be feeling.

What do you think your partner is trying to communicate in this instance? Perhaps some of your partner's needs aren't being met, such as the need for companionship, unconditional love, or support. The simplest way to calm down an angry or upset partner is by letting him or her understand you are hearing and accepting all his or her needs. Most of the problems in a relationship can be sorted through open and honest communication. If your partner feels heard and understood, chances are he or she will calm down instantly. Another person's chances of becoming defensive are quite high when he or she believes he or she is not being heard or is being ignored.

Step Two: Empathize

The second step of this technique is to empathize with your partner. Empathy is the ability of an individual to place him or herself in the shoes of another person. Instead of viewing things solely from your perspective, it's time for a paradigm shift. Every situation can be looked at differently depending on the perspective. Don't close yourself off to emotional responses, and instead, allow yourself to experience what your partner must be feeling in that instant. Once you believe you understand what your partner is feeling, check with your partner, and pay attention to his or her feelings. Notice what you feel when you observe your partner's feelings.

It's essential to reach deep into your heart and look for tender feelings of love and affection. Remember that whenever a person is acting out, superficial actions are triggered by an issue that isn't always visible. For instance, whenever a person feels hurt, upset, sad, or lonely, he or she tends to become defensive. These unpleasant emotions often manifest themselves as anger. Instead of reacting to your partner's anger, it is better to consider that his or her reactions stem from a painful or unpleasant emotion.

Do you stay in the present when your partner is talking to you? If not, it is time to concentrate only on the present. Don't allow any of your past experiences to guide your responses in this situation. Forget about any heated words that were exchanged. Instead, try to dig deep and reconnect with your partner. Try to experience the pain your spouse might be experiencing, which is manifesting itself as anger. Learn to be compassionate, and let your partner know that his or her experience of anger, sadness, or any other uncomfortable emotions is affecting you, too.

Whenever you notice that your partner is in distress, it's a natural human tendency to offer advice or suggestions to solve the problem. You might be doing this out of the goodness of your heart. However, this kind of advice is often viewed as criticism or can even come across as judgmental. If your partner perceives these things, it merely worsens the situation. Instead of falling into this vicious cycle of negativity, it's better to break free of the cycle. The simplest way to do this is by expressing compassion and showing empathy. Instead of advising your partner about what he or she should do, merely listen. At times, all that we need is to be heard. By listening to your partner's problems without interrupting, you are essentially conveying, "It is okay to feel whatever you are feeling. I am here for you." This simple message can easily prevent a tense situation from spinning out of control.

Step Three: Act

The third step of this process is to act. Now that you have understood what your partner is saying and feeling, it is time to address his or her concerns. While addressing such concerns, don't forget to show your willingness to change, if required. This step is all about an intentional commitment and an action that helps address your partner's needs, which were previously overlooked or ignored.

For instance, if your partner was upset that you don't usually help around the house, a simple way to show you are willing to address concerns and are willing to change is by helping your partner around the house. Instead of waiting for your partner to tell you what you're supposed to do, become proactive, and offer to do a specific household chore. It could be something as simple as doing the dishes after your spouse cooks a meal or putting away the laundry. When it comes to love and relationships, the small gestures often matter more than the grand ones. As you go about your day, take a couple of moments to type out a simple message, or place a quick call to your partner to say you are thinking about him or her. If your partner is anxious about your finances, why don't you start spending less to ease his or her anxiety? In a relationship, it's never about a single person. It is a two-way street, and unless both of you commit yourselves to the relationship, problems cannot be resolved.

By empathizing with your partner, you are showing that his or her feelings are valid and that you are willing to change. When push comes to shove, you are supposed to act on whatever message you have conveyed in the previous steps. By taking small steps, you can show that you take your partner's concerns very seriously and are willing to work towards making him or her feel more respected and valued. These simple tips help create a positive cycle in your relationship that can easily replace any existing negative patterns. Remember that perfection is not the key here. Instead, it's all about trying and showing your effort. By showing your willingness to change, you are essentially validating your partner's feelings and concerns. This simple gesture is sufficient to diffuse even the most unpleasant of arguments.

Step Four: Love

The final step of this technique is to feel and experience unconditional love. In a healthy relationship, love needs to be unconditional. If love becomes conditional, it increases the chances of a dysfunctional relationship.

If either one of the partners in a relationship starts believing that love is conditional, it will create more negative feelings. The simplest way to feel and experience unconditional love is by deliberately reconnecting with your partner and emphasizing loving feelings instead of unpleasant interactions. Remember that even if most of your recent interactions have triggered

Love: Fall In Love Again

unpleasant emotions in both of you, these things can be worked upon. Unless you work on this, all the effort you made in the previous steps will be undone.

The simplest way to reconnect with your partner is by reminiscing. In the previous chapters, you were given different practical tips you can use to reminisce about the good things about the relationship. It's not just you, but even your partner needs to do the same as you can take some time to think about the initial days of the relationship and the original qualities that attracted you to each other. You can look at old photographs, visualize any shared past experiences, or even exchange compliments.

If you or your partner made any mistakes, learn to forgive each other. Instead of living in the past and allowing it to overshadow a good future, it's better to deal with it. "Forgive and forget" is a great motto when it comes to maintaining a healthy relationship. If you believe you both can forgive each other, it becomes easier to move past mistakes. Once you move away from mistakes, ensure you both take corrective action to prevent these mistakes from reoccurring.

How would you define love? It could be defined as your concern for your partner's wellbeing. It has a warm and tingly sensation, which makes the world look beautiful and pleasant. Instead of allowing your love to be dictated by your partner's reactions and behaviors, make your expressions of love unconditional. Be there for your partner, support and try to understand him or her, and ensure your love for your partner is unconditional. If you believe there are any unresolved trust issues between you, work on fixing them instead of dealing with the superficial symptoms of the problem. Another great way to work on any unresolved issues is by seeking proactive therapy. You will learn more about this in subsequent chapters.

Fairytales and movies might have made you believe relationships are all about the happily ever after – the moment the protagonists walk hand in hand into the beautiful sunset. In reality, you both need to work on creating your happily ever after. A relationship is like a dynamic dance routine. Depending on the tempo of the music, the dance pattern and the steps need to change. No two individuals are alike, and therefore, it's important to be sensitive towards each other's life histories and any current stress you are dealing with. If you don't pay attention to these things, it's quite likely you will constantly step on each other's toes and bump into each other. These things can easily disrupt your dance routine. Instead of doing all this, it's better to repair your relationship and rekindle the love. Using the simple technique discussed in this section, you can both walk away from negative patterns and replace them with positive and desirable ones.

Chapter Sixteen: Proactive Therapy

Perhaps you and your partner have been together for a while, and you believe you are in an extremely healthy relationship. After all, you do have regular date nights, have a well-established framework for open and honest communication, and equally share all the household responsibilities. Even after doing all these things, do you honestly believe you are doing everything you possibly can to maintain your relationship? If you think there is some scope for improvement, consider proactive therapy or counseling.

So, what is proactive counseling or therapy? The term proactive suggests taking action before something happens. Therefore, proactive counseling or therapy is when a couple actively seeks therapy before the relationship turns sour. This might make you wonder why a seemingly healthy relationship requires counseling when things are going well. You might also start thinking that therapy is essential only for couples who are in some trouble. Well, this is just a myth. Therapy isn't just for when things go wrong. Life is unpredictable, and the only way to deal with all the uncertainties it has in store for you is through preparation. Once you prepare yourself, it becomes easier to tackle life.

Benefits of Proactive Therapy

Here are a couple of benefits of proactive therapy, which may help change your mind about it.

Willingly Accept Responsibility

It's quite common for couples in a relationship to have some disagreements. One fine day, you and your partner disagree, and it is time for you to take responsibility for your actions. Let's assume the disagreement is over a straightforward task that you forgot to do. Your spouse had to do the dishes, and he or she forgot. If the relationship is quite strong and the couple is in a good place, this is a small lapse in memory and wouldn't be treated as a big deal. However, if the couple is not in a good place, it can become a major argument. Are you wondering why this happens? A seemingly happy relationship can be riddled with several unresolved issues and emotions, resentments, and plenty of negative thoughts towards the relationship or the partner. If all these things are ignored or left unresolved for too long, they will bubble up to the surface. Once these harsh emotions rise to the surface, even a minor argument or a mistake quickly escalates into a nasty argument.

With proactive therapy, the partners can learn about communicating all their feelings with one another openly and honestly. Even amid a disagreement or an argument, partners can learn to control their emotions and sort out the issue calmly. Proactive therapy teaches you to accept your mistakes and take responsibility for such actions. It also gives your partner the skills to keep an open mind to hear the apology you offer. Things that might become a significant obstacle for couples merely become a speed bump for those in proactive therapy.

Become Receptive

If you and your partner decide to go ahead with proactive therapy when your relationship is in a good stage, it becomes easier to keep an open mind towards your partner's perspective. In a way, you both become receptive to each other's opinions and points of view. Even if there are disagreements, you both can work together with a therapist to reach a neutral solution. You can also work through these issues without suppressing or repressing your emotions. The sad fact is that most couples often seek therapy when things start unraveling. If you go to therapy under duress, it becomes difficult to keep an open, caring, and loving mindset.

Damage Control

A great thing about proactive therapy is it helps you deal with a potential problem before it becomes an unmanageable crisis. When things are going well in a relationship, you might turn a blind eye to certain quirks or behaviors, which might become problematic later. For instance, when you are in a happy mood, nothing can irritate you. However, when you were already irritated about something, your partner's slightest disagreement can make you snap.

If you keep ignoring any potential problems that can become bigger issues later, the best way to deal with it is through proactive therapy. An example of a potential problem could be the constant need of a partner to please others at his or her own expense. For instance, you might try to constantly please your partner by placing his or her needs over your own. You might also compromise on things you don't want merely to please your partner. During the happy stage, you might not think of it as a problem. After all, what marriage could survive without a few compromises? If the compromises are always made by one person while the other keeps demanding, the marriage will run into trouble. To avoid all this, seek proactive therapy. You and your partner might not notice that these patterns that exist, but the therapist will.

Unconditional Support

With proactive therapy, you and your partner can learn a lot more about each other. During discussions, you might discover some things you never knew about your partner. When you both start learning new things, it becomes easier to be more supportive and understanding. By discussing your strengths and weaknesses, fears and hopes, and dreams and aspirations with each other without any judgment, strengthening the relationship becomes easier. Remember that even the best of relationships needs a little help from time to time. Proactive therapy is the best help you can turn to.

Proactive therapy provides a chance for the partners in a relationship to understand that you both have each other's back. A relationship automatically becomes quite strong when the partners realize they each love and support the other unconditionally.

Seeking Feedback

With proactive therapy, it becomes easier to open yourself up for any feedback you receive. The counselor or the therapist you work with is a neutral third party whose sole purpose is to help you and your partner deal with each other's emotions and learn to manage them before they start controlling your marriage. By obtaining feedback from a neutral party, it becomes easier to fix any communication issues you might have never noticed before.

How Does Proactive Therapy Work?

A marriage cannot be free from conflicts, and learning to manage them is the only way you can reduce any damage they cause. To avoid or reduce the chances of any miscommunication or misunderstanding, it's important for the partners in a marriage to exert effort towards this goal consciously. When all these things are left unchecked, it can quickly unravel the marriage and lead to unnecessary altercations. If you want to reap all the benefits discussed until now, proactive therapy is the way to go. It helps couples build a deeper understanding of each other.

If a marriage is like a building, the foundation matters more than anything else. Regardless of how beautiful the facade is or how high the structure will be, if the foundation isn't strong, everything will crumble. The same holds true for marriage as well. There are some cornerstones for a successful marriage: mutual trust, unconditional love and acceptance, support, honesty, and good communication. Once all these ingredients are present in your marriage, it becomes easier to strengthen the bond you share with your partner.

Proactive therapy is a step-by-step process that helps fortify a marriage. The first step in therapy is assessing and analyzing the problems you might have as a couple that haven't been acknowledged yet. Even if a couple cannot see any major problems in the marriage, the therapist can be quite helpful. The therapist acts as a neutral third party, and his or her inputs can help the couple circumvent even the most minor of problems. If there are any arguments where you or your partner feel hurt, mistreated, or misunderstood, it kickstarts a vicious cycle of hurt. Instead of getting stuck in the cycle, with proactive therapy, a couple can finally analyze the problem, deal with it, and discover its cause. Instead of dealing with the unpleasant symptoms, proactive therapy helps strengthen the marriage by tackling the real issues.

Based on the therapist's findings and the partners' personalities, a plan of action that works well for everyone involved can be devised. From using simple couple games to monitoring behavior and educating partners about decoding each other's intentions, proactive therapy is quite helpful. Its primary aim is to strengthen the mutual bond by concentrating on common rituals and interests a couple can enjoy to renew their sense of togetherness. While having fun with each other, a couple can easily discover ways to rekindle the love in their relationship. Some common issues that can be resolved through proactive therapy include ineffective communication, growing distance between partners, annoyance because of trivial issues, the lack of trust, financial stress, dishonesty, loss of intimacy, family stress, and disinterest.

Here are the different skills proactive therapy can teach you that will come in handy while strengthening your relationship.

An important aspect of proactive therapy is communication. Communication is the only way in which one individual can convey his or her ideas, opinions, interests, experiences, feelings, and emotions to another. If a barrier creeps in, it becomes incredibly difficult to communicate. If you and your partner cannot communicate openly and honestly, it will create unnecessary issues later. Learning to talk respectfully and lovingly without any inhibitions is important. Remember that marriage is a long-term commitment, and unless you can freely talk to the other person, staying in the marriage becomes difficult. While communicating, proactive therapy suggests that you maintain eye contact, hold each other's hands whenever possible, and maintain pleasant facial expressions.

It's not just about communicating, but therapy also teaches you to be a good listener. Unless you listen to what the other person is saying without judgment, you cannot fully understand what he or she is saying. By simply listening to your partner, you can make him or her feel like you understand and empathize with him or her.

Proactive therapy also teaches you to love your partner the way he or she is. Instead of molding your partner to suit your idea of perfection, it teaches you to love him or her with his or her flaws. Remember those days during the initial phases of the relationship, when your spouse was the embodiment of perfection to you? Start remembering those days again. You loved your partner once, despite his or her flaws, and it would do you good to remember the same now. Once you accept your partner the way he or she is, it becomes easier to love him or her for all the good and joy he or she brings into your life.

While teaching you how to communicate positively with each other, proactive therapy also teaches you how to control your emotions. Unless you govern your emotions, your entire life will be guided by them. This is nothing more than a recipe for disaster. If you cannot control your emotions during an argument, things will easily spin out of control. It also teaches you to be there for each other. Unless you offer unconditional love and support for your partner, you cannot expect the same in return. Proactive therapy teaches couples about all the brilliant aspects of a relationship while helping them deal with any problems they might face. Once these troubles are addressed, it helps strengthen the bond.

Proactive marriage therapy helps you resolve conflicts healthily, develop good communication skills to foster a strong relationship, and express your needs without resorting to anger or getting excessively emotional. It also teaches you about the simple art of learning to forgive and forget. Apart from this, proactive therapy teaches you to be assertive without being aggressive, offensive, or disrespectful. It helps you process and work through any unresolved issues in a safe environment and creates an honest environment that's conducive to the growth and development of a relationship. With proactive therapy, you get a better understanding of yourself, your partner, and the relationship.

With proactive therapy, you and your partner can finally quit the blame game and objectively conceptualize your relationship. It teaches you that you both are a unit, and whatever happens to the relationship happens to not just one partner but to the two of you. It helps change your perspective towards the relationship, and it takes on a more positive view. Any dysfunctional behavior identified by the therapist during therapy can be easily rectified. Instead of waiting for a final outburst, proactive therapy helps modify such undesirable behaviors before they spin out of control. From substance use disorders to anger management, trust issues, or even manipulation, different dysfunctional behaviors can be easily identified with therapy.

By learning all the skills taught by proactive therapy, it becomes easier to control the issue or a situation before it arises. When two different personalities in a relationship come together, there can be a clash of ideas, opinions, perspectives, and mindset. The therapist helps strengthen the bond in the marriage by helping the partners understand they are independent entities, but they are also a unit in the relationship. You and your partner get an opportunity to analyze yourselves and each other, as well as understand the different aspects of your lives that need to be changed. It teaches you practical ways to help yourself and your partner create a happy and lasting marriage. By maintaining a level-headed approach, it becomes easy to reduce any discord in the relationship. It also helps identify any triggers or stressors, which might increase the strain on your shared bond.

Marriage takes work. However, the effort that goes in is not the same as mopping the floor or doing the dishes. The effort you put in to make a relationship work can be joyous, exciting, and even downright therapeutic. Don't view it as a chore, and making an effort certainly becomes easier. If you want to strengthen your relationship and obtain all the different benefits discussed in this section, consider the option of proactive therapy.

Sofia Price

Chapter Seventeen: Creating Emotional Safety and Security

"Why don't you ever share anything with me?"

"You could have told me!"

"Why are you always so quiet whenever I try to talk to you?"

"Why are you so secretive?"

"Why don't you ever talk about what you feel?"

Do these lines sound familiar to you? Okay, let's consider another scenario. You probably shared whatever you were feeling, and your partner quickly becomes defensive. Did you end up responding with, "This is the reason I didn't share it with you," "This is not what I meant," "I cannot have an honest discussion with you," or, "I shouldn't have even said anything in the first place." Do these responses sound familiar to you? If you or your partner have had such exchanges, chances are you need to look at the emotional intimacy quotient in your relationship.

Emotional intimacy is the freedom to express yourself in the relationship. This is the precondition required for safety and security. Safety and security aren't limited to physical aspects.

Here are the different ways safety and security are expressed in a relationship.

- Express yourself freely, and be your authentic self.

- The ability to share your insecurities and fears without worrying about judgment.

- The freedom to share your intimate desires, displeasure, and fantasies.

- Expressing your feelings and emotions about something your partner did, which upset you.

- Having conversations about difficult issues or topics without it turning into an argument.

The safety or security to share your thoughts or feelings in a relationship means saying or doing things without being subjected to name-calling, shaming, blaming, or rejection. Emotional safety means you can do all these things without being invalidated or even dismissed by your partner. Unless this level of safety and security exists in a relationship, you both cannot thrive together.

You cannot control what others feel. However, you can take responsibility for how you feel and how you present yourself in the relationship. For instance, if your partner says, "I cannot talk to you," maybe it's time to reconsider your behavior. Knowingly or unknowingly, most of us put up walls to prevent others from getting to know us. Perhaps you are dismissive and haven't even realized it. A little self-introspection at this stage gives a better understanding of your behavior. It doesn't mean you need to blame yourself when things go wrong. Instead, it merely means you are mature and now off to understand your mistakes and learn from them. In this section, let us look at tips for building and improving emotional safety, security, and intimacy.

Techniques to Build Emotional Safety and Security

Listen Without Judgment

Whenever your partner talks to you about their feelings and emotions, listen and validate them. Often, people don't share their vulnerabilities because they are worried about being misunderstood. After all, who would want to share if others are merely going to understand or blame them wrongly? The fear of being dismissed is quite real. Not many feel comfortable being vulnerable, and that is fine. Even if you cannot be empathetic towards your partner, make it a point to listen without any judgment. Try to create a safe and open space in the relationship so that you both can communicate with each other without the fear of judgment. The real problem starts when you start getting defensive. If your partner is telling you he or she was upset about something you did or said, it's not the time to get defensive. Instead, allow your partner to talk. After your partner is done, try to introspect about what might have gone wrong. The relationship isn't just about a single person. One person cannot be wrong.

Do not dismiss your partner, don't blame your partner for what he or she is feeling, and certainly don't change the subject. Instead, learn to empathize with your partner, don't make any judgment or comment, and validate your partner's feelings. Instead of you both internalizing your feelings, expressing them helps solve half the problems in the relationship. When you can both be vulnerable, it brings emotional intimacy.

Work on Commitment

Some reactions, such as asking for a divorce, ending the relationship, or even withdrawing, are absolutely undesirable. What can be more damaging than instances when you completely shut off your partner or wish to end the relationship? If both the partners react like this, the relationship cannot survive. These two behaviors can make the other partner feel disregarded, insecure, and unsafe, and it can trigger any abandonment issues your partner has. For instance, if you keep saying, "I want a divorce," every time you argue, sooner or later, it will make your partner feel insecure about the relationship. If you are both in a happy relationship, never toss the D-word around. If you cannot create a safe space when you and your partner can figure things out together as a team, it doesn't make any sense. You have both committed to each other, and it's vital to work on this commitment. After all, commitment is the thing that keeps you going when things start getting tough.

Instead of blaming each other, it is better to use "I" statements to express what you feel. When it comes to dealing with the issue, always consider yourself a team, and project this by using "we" statements. Follow the simple techniques that were discussed in the previous chapters about dealing with arguments.

Body Language Matters

Communication is of two types. We use verbal and non-verbal communication to express our ideas, emotions, feelings, and so on. Your body language matters a lot because it accounts for a significant part of non-verbal communication. More than words, we often rely on our body language, gestures, facial expressions,

Love: Fall In Love Again

body movements, and others to convey our messages. You might not pay much attention to it, but your body language conveys a lot. For instance, if you say, "I'm fine," while you are frowning and the corners of your mouth are turned down, what does it imply? Even though your words are conveying a message, your body language is suggesting you are visibly upset.

During an argument, avoid pointing fingers at each other. Yes, the physical act of pointing a finger at another person is viewed as aggressiveness. Also, don't cross your arms, don't walk away from the conversation, maintain pleasant or at least neutral facial expression, or sigh dejectedly during such conversations. If you do any of these things, it will make your partner feel worse than before and make you look dismissive. These things will further worsen the situation. So, what can be done? Maintain eye contact whenever you are talking to your partner. If you cannot smile, at least maintain a neutral facial expression, touch your partner's hand while talking, show your partner that he or she has your attention, and don't create any unnecessary physical space between you both.

Start being mindful of your body language. There are many things you can alter about yourself, but your body language always betrays your intentions. Also, if there is any discord between the words you speak and your body language, it can confuse your partner. Therefore, start paying attention to your body language, especially during trying circumstances. For instance, if your partner is visibly upset about something and is crying, don't walk away. Instead, sit by your partner's side, offer a comforting hug, or simply hold your partner's hand while he or she talks. These simple gestures show that you are not only willing to understand what your partner is saying but are also there for him or her. This is the kind of comfort everyone craves for. Once again, it's not just you who needs to do everything, but even your partner needs to commit him or herself to the relationship. Once you are both on the same page about the kind of things you desire from each other, communication becomes easy, and chances of misunderstandings reduce.

Learn to be Consistent

As mentioned previously, your body language needs to be consistent with your verbal communication. Any discord creates unnecessary confusion and misunderstandings. The same rule applies to different aspects of your life and marriage. You need to be consistent if you want to build trust in the marriage. Consistency should be there in the words you say and all your actions. Once you know what to expect, it becomes easier to count on your partner. For instance, if you tell your partner you will be doing something, ensure you complete the task by the given deadline. It could be something as simple as folding the laundry in the evening or doing the dishes after dinner. No matter what the task is, prove to your partner that you are consistent. If you say something and never follow through, it makes you look inconsistent. It also makes your partner hesitant. After all, how can you trust someone who doesn't keep promises?

This kind of inconsistency also creates emotional distance and breaks the trust in the relationship. Instead, if you make promises and don't follow through but are extremely loving and nurturing to your partner one day and the opposite of that the following day while you tell your partner you are available for him or her at all times but are unavailable when he or she needs you, it creates inconsistency. Over a period, these small inconsistencies can erode the emotional intimacy in a relationship. This inconsistency can also cause unnecessary anxiety and stress.

Be Grateful

No matter what your partner says or how bad the circumstances are, be grateful to your partner for opening up to you. Opening up to a person is never easy. Let go of any walls you have put up because showing your vulnerabilities takes strength. Sharing such vulnerabilities with another individual can make you feel emotionally and mentally naked. If someone comes to you and shares his or her problems with you, it means this person trusts you and knows he or she will not be dismissed even after sharing information.

This trust is quite fragile, and once it breaks, you cannot put it back together. Therefore, whatever your partner says, no matter how it makes you feel, it would be better to thank your partner for sharing it with you. Let your partner know you appreciate what he or she shared and are grateful because you got a chance to learn more about him or her. Whether you agree or disagree, the only thing that matters in this situation is the trust you share. Unless you trust your partner, you cannot bare your soul to him or her. Trust comes with the knowledge that regardless of all the secrets shared, the other person will not use them to hurt you.

If you don't acknowledge your partner when he or she is vulnerable or shares something difficult, it will make your partner feel invalidated. Do not change the conversation, and certainly don't try to tell your partner that his or her worries, fears, or anything he or she said isn't important. Don't do anything to make your partner feel like you don't care. Any negative or dismissive comments you make at this stage, especially when your partner feels quite vulnerable, can be quite damaging.

Instead, learn to be encouraging. If your partner shares something with you, tell your partner you appreciate the trust he or she has in you and the faith in the relationship. After this, you should also acknowledge the fact that being vulnerable isn't easy, and you appreciate the gesture. You don't have to offer any advice or solutions. If your partner has a problem, wait until he or she explicitly asks you for some help. Usually, people want someone to talk to, so be there for your partner.

No Toxic Thoughts

There should be no toxicity in a relationship. If you have any toxic labels in your head about your partner, it's time to let them go. You might believe your partner is stubborn, judgmental, sensitive, weak, and aggressive, or so on. Any label you have in your head, erase it. Learn to be open to the relationship and your partner. With time, people change. Instead of jumping to conclusions and believing, "He thinks like this because he is extremely sensitive," give your partner the benefit of the doubt. We are all entitled to different emotions and often process feelings differently. How you handle your feelings isn't the same as how your partner does. As we are all different, extending this basic courtesy to each other is quite important. Whenever you notice a toxic thought about your partner, replace it. If you are unable to replace it, talk to your partner about it. Instead of holding on to a preconceived notion about your partner, talking it out helps.

If you start believing your partner isn't capable of change and are stuck holding on to the toxic labels, it will make you feel distant. You cannot have a positive conversation if you don't benefit from the doubt. You are not a telepath, so you cannot read your partner's mind. Instead of jumping to conclusions, talking about what you feel is better.

Tips to Improve Emotional Intimacy

Emotional intimacy is not just crucial for your marriage but also for your overall wellbeing. Different things can slowly erode emotional intimacy in a relationship; these include work stress, tensions of daily life, physical distance, any major changes, and so on. If emotional intimacy slowly goes away from the relationship, the day is not far when you wake up one fine morning and feel quite distant from your partner.

Emotional intimacy is as important as physical intimacy in a relationship. Usually, it's the so-called good things in life that slowly reduce emotional intimacy. For instance, a promotion at work is a good thing. However, it means working longer hours, fewer holidays, and more work. These things take away the emotional bond you share with your partner. If you are constantly preoccupied with several other things, you cannot concentrate on your partner or the relationship. This is one of the reasons why it's essential that all couples, regardless of the length of the relationship, concentrate on maintaining this bond. Are you wondering how you can do this? Well, here are some simple yet brilliant ideas that will rekindle your emotional bond.

Meaningful Activities

A simple way to improve emotional intimacy in a relationship is by spending quality time together. One way to do this is through date nights. Scheduling and maintaining date nights is good. However, if it becomes a routine or monotonous activity, it doesn't add value to your life or relationship. For instance, on date nights, if you both could go fancy restaurant to sit across the table from each other but are continually checking your emails, social media, or talking about your child's life, it doesn't make any sense. You are not spending time with each other. Instead, you are using the date night to do other activities.

Therefore, it's important to spend some time to indulge in activities that help deepen the connection you both share. Such activities help concentrate on each other as individuals and give you a chance to reconnect with each other. For instance, you could go for a long drive and get ice cream, join a baking class, or even go hiking. Remember that a change of setting doesn't make any difference when it comes to hashing out any differences. It doesn't matter whether you are at a nice restaurant or in the kitchen if all you are doing is talking about different stressors. Instead, spend some time together doing activities that help rekindle the emotional intimacy you share.

Being Available

To instantly elevate the emotional intimacy in your relationship, make a conscious decision always to be available to your partner. Aside from just being physically available, think of new ways in which you can be available for him or her. No, you shouldn't do this because you are supposed to or because you feel like owe your partner something. Do this because you can, and you want to. For instance, if you don't like doing the laundry, you could surprise your partner by saying, "Honey, let me do it today." It doesn't have to be a grand gesture. After all, a happy and healthy marriage is always about the little things. Go out of your way once in a while, and your partner will certainly appreciate your efforts. In fact, it increases your partner's willingness to reciprocate the same. A little generosity in the form of a pleasant surprise instantly increases the intimacy in the relationship.

Don't Stop Being Curious

Human beings are naturally curious. However, with age, most of us tend to let go of this childlike curiosity. If you want to grow in life, you need to learn. The simplest way to start learning is by being curious. Most of us are often quite rigid about our opinions and believe in being right more than understanding what the other person is feeling. Once you stop doing this and start paying attention to what your partner is saying and why he or she behaves the way he or she does, it becomes easier to understand your partner.

Curiosity isn't the same as the lack of boundaries. Learn to understand the difference between healthy curiosity and being nosy. If your partner talks about his or her childhood, ask questions that will make him or her open up. This is a sign of healthy curiosity.

When you are curious about the other person and wish to understand the reasons for his or her feelings without feeling threatened, it helps build empathy. You can do this without giving up on your own opinions and standing. Learning and understanding others doesn't mean giving up on your beliefs.

Instead, it merely means making more space in your heart and mind for your partner. Just making an effort to understand your partner doesn't mean you have to agree on everything. Even if you don't see eye to eye, you get a better perspective of the situation by understanding your partner. It also helps reduce any misunderstandings and arguments. Even if you disagree, it shows that you both care and love each other enough to try and understand the other's perspective.

Don't Give Up on Yourself

If two strong individuals come together, it automatically results in a strong relationship. It entirely depends on you to determine which direction the relationship goes. Being with someone doesn't mean giving up on yourself. Never let anyone tell you otherwise. Investing in yourself is important before you think about investing in the relationship. After all, if you are not 100% happy on your own, you cannot contribute to the relationship. If you give up on yourself, it will ultimately take a toll on your relationship, too.

When you are in touch with your feelings, needs, dreams, and desires, it strengthens your resolve, increases your self-confidence, and motivates you internally to keep going. All these positive attributes reflect on the health of a relationship. If you are riddled with self-doubt and constantly second-guess yourself, it will also poorly show on your relationship.

Every partner in a relationship should invest in his or her own overall health and wellbeing. When you feel your best, you can do your best for the relationship. Appreciate yourself, the life you lead, and everything you have today. Learn to live your life mindfully and meaningfully. These practices automatically translate into the health of your relationship, too. Instead of believing the relationship to be a simple tool to make you feel whole, the moment you realize you are whole on your own gives immense strength. If you have ever traveled on an airplane, you will remember one of the instructions from their safety manual. It suggests you should always put your oxygen mask on before you try and help someone else. If you are in no condition to help yourself, you certainly cannot help anyone else. The same rules should be applied to every aspect of your life. Therefore, concentrate on your mental, emotional, and physical wellbeing.

Learn to be Brave

Avoiding an issue, repressing emotions, or turning a blind eye towards problems gradually kills intimacy. When you don't address any concerns, whether it's an individual or mutual one, it reduces intimacy. For instance, you and your partner had an unpleasant conversation, which quickly spiraled into a heated argument. During the argument, in the heat of the moment, strong words were exchanged. It probably hurt you both, and you both regret saying certain things. However, if you don't revisit the conversation and try to address what went wrong, it's quite likely that the same scenario will occur again. Meanwhile, you both might be harboring unpleasant thoughts about the other and the relationship, too.

If you don't address such problems, they quickly spiral out of control or gain momentum over a period. You are probably aware of how volcanoes work. Due to the buildup of excessive pressure in the Earth's crust, the pressure seeks a way out. This way out is how a volcano erupts. To prevent such an eruption, it's important to reduce the stress or the pressure that builds up. The same rule applies to your relationship, too. If you keep avoiding issues or don't address any concerns you or your partner might have, sooner or later, they all bubble up to the surface. Dealing with a simple issue is easier than dealing with multiple issues at once. To avoid any unpleasantness, it's important to be brave and have those discussions when required.

At times, it is a good idea to shelve a topic until it's the right time. For instance, when you feel tired and annoyed, it isn't the right time to discuss finances. When you're both calm, you can put your heads together and plan to manage your finances. However, in the long run, avoidance has the same effect elements, similar to the effect wind and water have on rocks. It takes time, but the sharp edges of the rocks slowly change. The same happens in your relationship, too. The erosion occurs daily, but it isn't noticeable until after time passes.

Having difficult conversations is not easy. It can bring up a lot of unpleasant issues and scenarios you probably don't even want to deal with. Think of it as stripping a Band-Aid. The sooner you rip it off and the more quickly you do it, the less it hurts. However, if you take longer, the more painful the process becomes. This is where bravery comes into the picture. Learn to be brave, and tackle these issues head-on. Sweeping them under the rug or turning a blind eye doesn't solve them. Pretending like the issues don't exist merely worsens the situation. It also takes a certain degree of strength to showcase this kind of vulnerability.

Being vulnerable is often mistaken as a weakness. Vulnerability is not the same as weakness. In a good relationship, both partners have the freedom to be vulnerable without worrying about judgment or repercussions. In fact, there shouldn't be any repercussions for being vulnerable. If you can express all your fears and doubts without worrying about what the other person thinks, it becomes easier to address them. Usually, these fears and doubts are worse in your head than they are. By sharing them, it takes away the power they have over you.

One thing you need to keep in mind while having such conversations is that you shouldn't be aggressive. There is a difference between being brave and being aggressive. If you are aggressive, it can make your partner retreat, withdraw, or be resentful. None of these things are desirable. Aggressiveness also quickly ends any fruitful conversation you both can have. If you keep your calm, talk about the issue rationally and logically, and behave maturely, all issues can be resolved. When you overcome a problem by working together as a team, it increases the intimacy you experience. It gives you both the courage and confidence that you can count on each other's support and tackle the problem, regardless of how bad things get.

Create A "Nice" List

It is quite easy to find faults in others. Focusing on each other's flaws increases resentment and will ultimately take away the love from the relationship. We are all flawed, and once you start looking for flaws, stopping becomes difficult. Therefore, don't look for flaws; instead, look for positive points. Take a couple of minutes and sit down with your partner. Start creating a gratitude list. Try writing in detail about different qualities you both appreciate in the other. It could be as simple as, "I love how you hug me as soon as I get home." You don't have to think about anything major. If you cannot think of any characteristics, per se, start writing down what your partner does that makes you feel loved and wanted. This simple exercise helps you reconnect and understand why you fell in love in the first place.

Sofia Price

Chapter Eighteen: Rekindling Your Passion

Experts say that couples always lose their passion when they stop being intimate. They need to ensure that they continue to have sex, regardless of what the situation may be. In this chapter, we will look at some tips to help you rekindle your passion.

Fostering Emotional Intimacy

Any relationship is built on closeness and emotional intimacy. You can expect to have a good sexual relationship if you and your partner are close to each other. In simple words, if you want to improve your physical intimacy, you should first work on developing an emotional connection with your partner. You must ensure that you communicate and meet the needs of your partner. Do this respectfully and lovingly. Dr. Gottman, in his book *The Science of Trust*, says that a couple that wants to rekindle love and passion must always turn toward each other. You can stay connected to your partner even when you have a difference of opinion because of emotional attunement. You need to show him or her empathy and not be defensive. You and your partner should talk about your feelings. Make sure you understand what your partner needs.

Dr. Gottman also states that when partners express a positive need, the relationship will succeed. You and your partner should listen and speak with each other so you can convey requests and complaints without fearing being judged or blamed. Gottman also says that partners should stop blaming each other. They should not think about what is wrong with their partner but should understand what they can do to help their partner. Understand that when your partner talks to you, he or she is telling you that he or she is feeling a certain way, and he or she needs you to be there for him or her.

Rekindling Sexual Chemistry

Couples will never come up for air when they are newly married. They are excited about falling in love. This state does not last forever, and you must understand this better. The bonding hormone, oxytocin, is released when partners are in the initial stages of infatuation. This will make couples feel turned on and euphoric. Even the slightest touch will make it hard for new couples to keep their hands off each other. This hormone works like a drug. It will allow couples to bind themselves.

Hugs, tender touches, holding hands, and other similar gestures are the easiest way to let your partner know that you love him or her. When you show them affection physically, it will set the stage for sexual touch. This is focused only on pleasure. Dr. Michael Stysma, a sex educator and therapist, states that you should always increase the time you hug, kiss, or even touch. This is a good way to improve your marriage.

It is hard to maintain sexual attraction over time. Let us look at some tips that will help you improve your sexual chemistry.

Initiate Sex Differently

You are probably coming on too strong or maybe denying your partner any pleasure. Never play the blame game. You also need to ensure that you do not criticize each other. Try to mix stuff up and end the struggle. For instance, some couples will choose to initiate sex a lot more often. Others will find a way to let their partner know that they feel sexy. They will do this in subtle ways and while demanding some closeness.

Hold Hands

According to Dr. Kory Floyd, a psychologist, and author, touching, holding hands, and hugging will release the hormone oxytocin in your mind. This will lead to a calming sensation. Research and studies show that this hormone is released when you have an orgasm. Remember that physical affection will help to reduce stress. This will lower the production of cortisol, the stress hormone.

Let the Tension Build

Your brain will experience a lot of pleasure during sex. It will experience even more pleasure when you anticipate sex. You need to let your partner anticipate what you will do in bed. Make sure that you spend some time during foreplay. Entice your partner, and arouse him or her. You should change locations, learn more about his or her fantasies, and use role-play.

No Routine

You should try to avoid discussing any household chores, office troubles, and relationship problems when you are in the bedroom. You need to plan intimacy time, but you need to ensure that you do not make this a routine. If you are too stressed or distracted, your sexual arousal will plummet.

Spend Time

You should always try to do different activities together. Make sure that you choose activities that bring both of you pleasure. You should flirt with each other, and try to court each other as a way to ignite sexual intimacy and desire. Gottman says that anything that you do that resonates positively with your partner can be foreplay.

Use Affection

You can always give your partner a shoulder rub or back rub. Remember that some people love foreplay since that will help them with having amazing sex. Affectionate touch is an amazing way to rekindle or even demonstrate passion. You should try to do this even when you are not an emotional person.

Love: Fall In Love Again

Be Emotionally Vulnerable

You should share your innermost fantasies, desires, and wishes with your partner, so he or she knows what you love during sex.

If you are scared of emotional intimacy, you need to engage in couple's therapy or even individual therapy.

Be Curious

You always need to find a new way to pleasure yourself. You need to learn more about your partner through sex. This is one of the easiest ways to learn more about your partner.

Improvise

You should always try something new when you have sex. You can have highly erotic, intimate, gentle, and loving sex. Always try doing something new, and break the routine. We will look at some different positions you can try to improve your sex life.

Always Make Sex a Priority

You must set the mood right before you start working or watching Netflix. Otherwise, these activities will dull your mood. You should have a light meal along with your favorite wine and music. This will set the stage for amazing sex.

You can also ask your partner to entice you because that will help to reignite the spark. This is an easy way to do this. Gottman says that you need to be friends with your partner if you want to ensure that the marriage works. If both partners know each other well and are well versed in each other's dreams, hopes, likes, dislikes, and personality quirks, you will make it. Even if you are someone who is not touchy-feely, you can increase your emotional attunement and physical affection to sustain a meaningful and deep bond.

Chapter Nineteen: The Passion Ignition Plan

When the relationship is new, you feel like you are on cloud 9. You often share intimate moments and make love often. You and your partner were attracted to each other physically and longed for passionate moments just as much as you enjoyed other aspects of being together. However, as time goes by, the passion seems to fizzle. You no longer touch or make love as often. You may even feel that at one point, you are no longer sexually attracted or connected to your partner. This could be because you have let yourselves go, or maybe you've grown insecure about your relationship, so you avoid being intimate with each other. If you want to fall in love with your partner again, you have to rediscover passion and intimacy in your relationship.

Below is a Passion Ignition Plan that will help you heat up your relationship and bring back excitement and passion.

Share a Fantasy with Your Partner

We all have a dirty sexual fantasy; this fact is what makes erotic books as successful as they are. To ignite the passion in your relationship, share your fantasy with your partner, and encourage your partner to do the same. It can be a turn on, and it can significantly improve your sex life. If you want to take the heat up a notch, you can act out those fantasies if, of course, you are comfortable with it. If you act on a sexual or erotic fantasy every once in a while, you will ignite the passion and spark in the relationship.

You may be concerned that your partner won't want to share with you or that you are too shy to make this work. Be open with each other. It's okay if you or your partner doesn't want to do something, or it doesn't feel pleasurable for one or both of you. If nothing else, sharing your fantasies with each other will get you thinking about new ways to ignite your passion. It can also help you discover new things about your partner while keeping your communication very honest and open.

Change Up the Sex Schedule

Most couples or spouses who have been in a relationship or marriage for a very long time often have a sexual routine or schedule. This could be the source of boredom. Change your sex schedule every now and then. This will spice up your relationship and rekindle the passion.

Be spontaneous! You have nothing to lose by making love in the morning instead of before you go to sleep. Ask your partner or spouse if he or she would like to be intimate when he or she gets home from work. Remember how we talked about surprising your partner? This could be a fun and sexy way to make your spouse or partner feel appreciated. Does your partner usually initiate the passion in your relationship? Shock your partner by making the first move! It may be uncomfortable for you to be so forward at first, but your partner will appreciate you wanting to bring the fire back to your relationship. Taking the initiative in the bedroom can also serve as a reassurance to your partner that you still desire him or her, especially when your partner may be feeling like you've lost the desire to be intimate.

Be Adventurous

If you are a rigid type, it is time to be more adventurous. Have public displays of affection with your partner every once in a while. You could also kiss and make out in a public place or have sex in unexpected places. Of course, follow this tip only if you are comfortable with it. If you are not comfortable making out in public or having sex in the car or an unexpected place, then that's perfectly okay.

Are you and your spouse or partner stuck in a rut where you have sex the same way every time? Change it up! There are countless websites, books, and magazines that can offer new and interesting ways to heat things up and make you both want to try something new. Once again, this is a great way to be open and communicate with your partner about what you are interested in and willing to try, as well as others that might not work for both of you. Being adventurous can be fun when you open up to each other and give it a chance.

Cuddle Every Morning

Couples often cuddle when the relationship is new. Try to cuddle again in the morning. Touching each other, hugging, and cuddling will significantly change how you feel about your partner. You will begin to reconnect with your partner physically and emotionally when you cuddle. If you want to keep the fire burning in your relationship, make cuddling a regular habit.

As we discussed earlier, physical touch can be something very important to some people. It can make them feel content and safe to be held by someone they love. Your partner may also want to provide these same feelings to you. Some people can sleep in their partner's arms all night long, while others might only have time to spoon and cuddle for a few minutes before their alarm goes off. In the instance that you and your partner work separate shifts and do not sleep at the same time, just an extended embrace will work wonders. When your partner is doing the dishes or working on the computer, just walk up behind your partner and wrap your arms around him or her. You never know what is going on in your partner's mind at that moment, and an affectionate embrace may be just what he or she needs. Either way, think of how nicely your day will start if you take the time to be affectionate with your partner or spouse. You could talk to each other during this special time, or you could sleep a little bit longer. It will make your relationship stronger.

Get Fit

It is highly recommended for couples to exercise together. Running or going to the gym together will give you time to be together, share an interest, have loads of fun together, and increase your attraction toward each other. These are all things that can help rekindle your relationship, and you'll be able to make yourself look good while working out things with your partner at the same time. It's a win-win for everyone!

Having your spouse or partner exercise with you can help you both be accountable. If you are both trying to lose weight to become the best version of yourself, it's far easier when you have someone who is supporting you and motivating you to get better. You can make working out fun. You can take a spin class or boot camp classes. You can spot each other while you learn how to lift weights. You don't even have to go to the gym at all to get fit. There are plenty of workout programs that can be done at home, whether they are a video or a video game. In the age of fitness apps on your phone and fitness watches, it's easy for you and your partner to work out without a gym or personal trainer. The world can be your gym if you and your partner like taking long walks or running.

It's good to keep other aspects of your relationship fresh and fun, and you can apply this to exercise. Keep changing your workout schedule. If you do something different every day, working out will continue to be fun and won't get boring as you continue to exercise. Do a workout class on a rainy day, and go for a jog when there is nice weather. Be open to new and fun ways to work out and get healthy together.

Kiss Your Partner Passionately for at least 10 Seconds Everyday

Just like it's important to spend time with your partner or spouse every day or to make sure that you make it a point to listen to what he or she has to say, it's also important to have some physical interactions with your partner, too. It doesn't necessarily have to be sex; something as simple as kissing your partner can add new fire to your relationship.

Kiss your partner passionately for at least 10 seconds every day; this is one way to reignite your passion and heat up your relationship. Kissing is both intimate and romantic. People often say that kissing is far more intimate than sex. Ten seconds of passionate kissing every day will help reawaken your old feelings and desires. There is nothing more romantic than sharing a passionate kiss before going to work or when you arrive home from work. Sharing a passionate kiss in those precious moments that you have alone with no worries not only reaffirms your affection for each other but could also lead to more intimate relations that have been lacking. Although it is recommended that you kiss your partner passionately daily for at least 10 seconds, there is no rule that you cannot go beyond 10 seconds. If you feel like kissing your partner for more than 10 seconds daily, go ahead and splurge. If you take the time to kiss your partner every day, it will eventually become a habit. This new habit benefits you both, and you and your partner will look forward to those special moments each day.

Intimacy is an important part of the relationship. If you want to fall in love with your partner all over again, you have to ignite the passion and intimacy. When you heat up your sex life, your relationship will feel like it is new again, and eventually, the boredom will go away.

Chapter Twenty: Love Is a Verb

Love is not a mere feeling. When you feel that your love for your partner is fading, maybe you have stopped doing loving things. Love, above all, is a verb. It is an action word. When you love someone, it is not enough that you feel it; you also have to show it.

It is easy to complain about the things that you do not like in your spouse or partner. It is easy to criticize your partner. However, to rekindle your relationship and reawaken the love and affection that you have for your partner, you also have to look inside yourself and reassess your behaviors and character. Do you have some basic beliefs about marriage, relationships, or your partner that could be feeding the difficulties and problems you currently have in your relationship?

While it is perfectly normal for you not to have the same beliefs or opinions as your partner or spouse, some topics can probably be considered as hot button issues. Is one of you more religious than the other? Perhaps you are two separate religions, or is one of you questioning your faith? If you are not on the same page or this view has changed since you first started your relationship, this can cause tension. This stance or point of view can also apply to how you and your spouse or partner feel about having children or parenting them. It could even affect the relationships you have with others outside of your relationship. Maybe you are having trouble feeling loved in this relationship because you are worried that you are not pleasing your partner or are curious to know what else is out there. These are all serious areas that you must both think about and address.

You have to communicate. Just like you made a point to tell your significant other how you felt about him or her, you need to do the same about these topics. Why does your partner feel the way he or she does, and if it has changed since you originally got together, can he or she tell you why? If your spouse or partner is feeling vulnerable about your relationship to the point where he or she is having thoughts of seeking out others or even accusing you of doing something similar, ensure your partner that this is not true. Is this something that you can find middle ground on? In the example of children, maybe one of you isn't ready to have children yet, but maybe you would be willing down the road once you are more financially stable or have had time to enjoy being together on your own without even more responsibilities. Let your spouse or partner know that you still love and support him or her even if he or she is becoming more or less religious, want to try different approaches to raising your children, or any other sort of situation that might be difficult for you both to agree on at first.

Actions speak louder than words. This can easily apply to the idea that love is a verb. To love someone is to try your hardest to show this person what he or she means to you. To love someone is to attempt to put his or her happiness before your own. To love someone means working hard to make a relationship work. While you need to listen to your partner despite these difficulties and problems, you must show your love and understanding of his or her feelings as well. Is your partner afraid that he or she hasn't had enough experiences with other people and is now feeling trapped in a relationship? Does your partner feel jealous or concerned that you are not showing enough attention and that you might be interested in someone else? Show your partner how you truly feel. While you can assure your partner with promises, it means so much more if you get rid of those

Love: Fall In Love Again

doubts by being a more attentive partner. Give your partner no reason to worry about another person.

As regards religion or life changes, support your partner. You don't have to change your beliefs, but commend your partner for his or her efforts, participate if you are comfortable, and show your partner that these changes will add more variety to your relationship. If you and your partner are working out the finer points of parenting or becoming parents, show patience, and remain involved. Help your partner with parenting ideas, and follow through on them. If something doesn't work out when you are taking care of your child, kindly offer suggestions of what could work instead.

As regards having children, show your respect if they aren't quite ready, but if you notice a moment that your partner seems interested in motherhood or fatherhood someday, you could make it a positive experience by complimenting your partner or assuring him or her of your support.

Couples do not stop being in love with each other. What couples do is they stop acting in love. As they do not act lovingly, feelings often start to fade away. It becomes easy to forget to show love to your spouse when you become wrapped up in other things. You just assume that your partner knows that you love him or her. Somewhere along the line, you become like friends or roommates because you aren't professing your love anymore. Just like you need to eat, sleep, and breathe, a person needs to be shown attention and affection. Just because you are in a committed relationship doesn't mean you have to stop acting like you love each other; if anything, you want to act more in love than ever. You both should feel happy and lucky that the other person loves you and wants to be with you!

If you want to be in a happy relationship, you have to take a good look at your character. You have to check if you have all the qualities that you want in a partner. You see, if you are falling out of love with your spouse or your partner, maybe your partner is not the only one who is at fault here. Maybe you have certain negative beliefs about your partner, about love, about relationships, and about marriage. If you want to be in a happy relationship or a happy marriage, you have to be the kind of person who vibrates warm and positive energy.

Life can be hard. It can be so easy to get down about things if you aren't where you want to be financially or if you have goals that you think should already be achieved that haven't been yet. You can't let yourself get down and become negative because that will impact other areas of your life, including your relationship. Maybe your negativity could be the reason why things are no longer the same as at the beginning of your relationship. Maybe you thought that all the quirks that your spouse or partner had back when you met would be fixed by now, and they're not, and you feel like you failed or that your significant other isn't trying. Maybe you thought that being in a marriage wouldn't change your life very much, and yet you find that your old life has vanished, and the responsibilities of your new life are not as thrilling as you'd hoped.

You have to try to find the positives. Negativity is like cancer or a black, dark vortex that grows and grows if you don't find a way to get rid of it. You are alive, and you have a spouse or partner who loves you and wants to be with you. That alone is a reason to be happy. If you turn all of those negative points into positive ones, you find a reason to be happier, and your relationship will become happier, too.

Love: Fall In Love Again

Just like you made a list of all the great things about your partner or spouse, do the same for yourself. Are you a great listener? Do you think you are really great at surprising your significant other and making him or her happy when you find the perfect gift or take your partner to a fun night out? Write down as many things as you can to remind yourself of how awesome you are. That will encourage you to be happy and positive. Remember, love is a verb. So, all of those things that you think you do well in your relationship? Do them. Shower your spouse with attention, and hold your partner's hand when he or she needs a reminder of your support. Give your partner a compliment when he or she looks great. Show your partner or spouse what you have to offer.

Remember the golden rule. Treat other people the way you want to be treated. If you want your partner to be kinder to you, show kindness to your partner. If you want passion in your relationship, be a passionate partner. If you want your partner to listen to you, listen to your partner often. If you want your partner to be loving, be a loving partner. This is so easy to do, and there is nothing negative that can come from putting yourself out there and setting the example. Maybe your partner has been wanting to be passionate or more affectionate around you but is afraid to because he or she doesn't think that you care or will reciprocate. By taking the high road or setting the tone, your partner will know that you feel the same way, and your relationship will burn anew because you want to be constantly pleasing and taking care of each other.

Love is not just some feeling; it is not just the electricity you feel in your veins. Love is not just about your heart beating fast when you are with your spouse or your partner. Love is caring for your partner when he or she is sick. Love is making your partner breakfast and kissing him or her before you both leave for work. Love is about saying kind words, even when you feel angry and annoyed. Love is making time for your partner. Love is giving your partner a gift that you know he or she would like. Love is about appreciating your partner.

Again, love is a verb, and doing little random acts of love is sure to rekindle your affection and love for your partner. Love takes work, and by no means is it easy. However, the feeling of knowing that you are providing happiness for another person so that he or she, in turn, would want to be with you is worth the effort.

Chapter Twenty-One: Enhancing Sex

In the last chapter, you learned that love is a verb. So, you need to learn to make sex more pleasurable for both of you. You need to ensure that you have a fit body if you want to have good sex. This chapter covers physical routines and movements that you can perform along with your partner so you can get fit together. This chapter will also shed some light on the different positions you can try to make your sex life more fun.

The Importance of Performing Physical Activities Together

Studies and research show that exercise is an aphrodisiac. A study conducted on ten people showed that eight out of ten people felt that exercise helped to boost their self-confidence. Out of those eight people, four were sexually aroused, and three out of those four people had sex frequently at home. Physical exercise helps to build strength and endurance, which has multiple benefits. You will benefit from strength when you try the different positions mentioned in this chapter. Exercise helps to increase blood flow, which gives you more energy, and this is important for sex. When you exercise together, you will learn to focus on your body and your partner's. This will help increase sensual awareness. Physical exercise also releases a hormone in the brain, which is also released during sex.

When you work out with your partner, you will find that it pays off immediately. As you are exercising, you will have a burst of adrenaline in your body. The love hormone – endorphin – and the happy hormone – oxytocin – are both released. This prepares your body to ensure pleasure during sex. Let us look at some exercises you can perform with your partner.

Pelvic Thrusts

The motions made by any person using the pelvic area generate the most powerful sexual energy. Learn to perform these thrusts alone. Make sure to perfect the movement before you do this with your partner. You also need to let your partner know that he needs to perform these thrusts himself, too. You should listen to music while you exercise, so you feel more energetic. Once you perfect the movement, you should ask your partner to do the exercise with you. This movement sounds very easy, doesn't it? You only have to thrust your pelvis forward and backward. This is, however, not true. Most human beings have a stiff pelvis and find it difficult to thrust. Stand with your feet shoulder width apart and tuck your abdomen in. Thrust your hip forward and backward. Start slowly, and then increase the pace. You have to keep your torso stiff and isolate your hips.

Stand facing each other. Play some soft music and start moving around. When you are comfortable, you should start thrusting at a low height. Continue to thrust while you move from standing up to lying down on your back. You can make this exercise more fun by adding some elements of surprise. You will feel the energy surging through your body. Make sure that the two of you exert yourself enough.

Dance

Most couples are shy when they are asked to dance together. It could be that they are conscious about how they look when they dance. When was the last time you and your partner danced? Did you dance when you went to the restaurant on a date? No, right? This is where you made a mistake. Dancing will make you feel more energetic. When you and your partner dance together, your bodies will move together. This will help to increase sexual energy. Do you remember the way Johnny and Baby danced? The sexual tension and energy between the two of them could not be missed. You will always have to pace your dance movements with your heart rate. You can start with slow, sexy, and sensual movements and then move into fast-paced movements. Let yourself go. Let your body move with the music.

Working Out in the Bedroom

Rundy Duphiney is a former professional athlete. He used to work out every day to ensure that he would stay fit. When he traveled to meet his partner, he would take a break from his workout. This worried him because he did not want to stop being fit. When he started to worry, he realized that he was being silly. He saw that he was working out quite a bit when he was with his partner. He then developed a routine that helped him stay fit even when he did not work out. This section covers the basic steps of the workout.

1. Face your partner in either the bedroom or the shower. Look into each other's eyes begin to roll your head from one shoulder to the next. Then stretch your body by leaning towards the opposite direction. If your partner is moving right, you will have to move left. Now, move your

arms in synchrony with your partner. This has to be done while facing each other. After rotating your arms, you must rotate your hips. Once you are both aroused, you need to turn around and let your partner face your back. Let him or her guide your pelvis, and move it away from his or her body. When you perform this exercise, you will tone your thighs and hips while your partner will tone his or her hips, stomach, thighs, and glutes.

2. The next exercise is the partner push up. Ask your partner to lie down on his or her back and raise his or her hips in the air. Your partner will work his or her lower back and abs. Now, lean over your partner, and support yourself with your arms. Now, slowly move over your partner by lowering and raising your body like you are doing a pushup. Once you do this, switch positions.

3. The next exercise is the simplest. Ask your partner to lie on his or her back and prop his or her knees up. Straddle your partner at his or her waist. Now, ask your partner to move his or her body upward and clutch your buttocks. Allow your partner to move your body upward and downward.

4. Sit up in the yab yum position, which is explained in the next section. Both of you should grab each other's wrists while the man is still inside the woman. Now, lean backward slowly and stay in the position for a few seconds. After a few seconds, you should move back to the first position. Repeat this at least ten times.

Basic Positions

In this section, we will look at some basic sex positions that are a great way for you to improve your sex life.

The Sidewinder

Inspired by a yoga position of the same name, the sidewinder is a technique that allows for deep penetration. It also allows for great eye contact. To perform the technique, the woman must lie on her side and support her upper torso with the help of her hand. One leg is lifted and placed on the man's shoulder with the other lying on the bed. The man sits on his knee between her two legs. An alternative is for the man to lay behind the woman and enter from behind. The woman's position remains the same.

The Yab Yum

Considered to be the best position for tantric sex, the yab yum allows both parties to garner simultaneous orgasms. Although fairly simple to perform, this position helps to hit all the right spots. It also allows for the man's hands to be free to do what they want, and the couple can kiss to glory. To perform this pose, the man must sit with his legs crossed and maintain a straight back. The woman sits on top of his legs and wraps her legs around his lower back. Slow up and down movements are made until both can reach a timed orgasm.

Time Bomb

Also known as the get down, this technique allows the woman to reach full penetration and is known as the best technique to hit the g-spot. The pose also allows for easy kissing. To perform this technique, the man must sit on a chair, preferably a straight back. The woman sits on his lap, facing the man, and lowers herself onto his lap. The woman can move up and down, or the man can move her up and down by placing his hands below her butt.

The Padlock

This pose allows the man to have a good look at the woman's face and upper torso and vice versa. It makes for a very sexy pose that helps pleasure both parties. To perform this technique, the woman must sit on a high platform like a table or kitchen counter. She must then lean back and balance her shoulder, neck, and head with the help of her elbows and arms. The man stands in between the legs and enters. His hands are free to do whatever.

The Butterfly

This technique is said to give both parties a high level of ecstasy owing to its quality of helping with deep penetration. To perform this technique, the woman must lie on a table in such a way that the butt lies at the very edge. The man must help the woman lift her lower back off the table and place her legs over his shoulders. How high the butt is lifted depends on the man's height. The man enters her with her butt in mid-air. The woman must twist her neck a little backward to counterbalance the pose.

The Double-Decker

This pose is extremely sexy and will almost always result in an orgasm. It allows the man a good view of what is going on down there and also frees his hands to play with her butt. This is a woman-in-charge pose. To perform this technique, the man must sit on the bed with his folded legs beneath his body. The woman faces the other way and places her feet on either side of the man with feet placed flat for support. The girl moves up and down or forward and backward, and the guy can do whatever with his hands.

The Hot Seat

The hot seat is a great pose to help reel in the right amount of pressure and give both parties an amazing sexual experience. Both parties have equal control in this move. To perform this pose, the man sits on the bed with his knees supporting his upper body and lower legs, placed backward and a little apart. The woman sits in the same position but facing the other way, with her butt pressing against his scrotum and back against his chest. Her legs are joined and placed in the space between his legs. The man enters from behind. The pose calls for both parties to stay as close as possible.

Rowboat

The rowboat is a slight twist on the woman-on-top pose. This pose helps position the bodies in such a way that both people can have a good look at each other's faces. To perform this pose, the man sits on a chair that has the capacity to bend backward. The woman sits on his lap and places her legs on the sides of the chair. The girl can move upwards and downwards by herself or have the man lift her and down by placing his hands beneath her butt.

The Mermaid

The mermaid is a changed version of the butterfly and allows a tighter grip and a better comfort level. The pose allows the man to play with the woman's feet, which is seen as an amazing erogenous spot. To perform this technique, the woman lies in the same position as that for the butterfly but with a pillow placed below her butt for support. Her legs are outstretched at a 90-degree angle, and the man stands very close to the table. The joining of legs allows for an extremely comfortable and tight grip.

Tidal Wave

This pose is so comfortable and sexy that it will blow your mind. This pose is a slight role reversal where the woman mimics the man's pose from the missionary position. To perform this technique, the man must lie flat on his back with his arms by his side. The woman sits on top and inserts his penis inside her all the way through. The girl must completely stretch out with legs resting on his legs. The girl's palms are placed on his forearm for support. The girl moves her pelvic region upward and downward to ride the man.

Lap Dance

This pose allows the man a great experience. He has free hands to do what he wants and has the woman facing his way. He also has a good view of his partner's face. To perform this pose, the man must sit on a chair with his back straight. The woman sits on his lap and balances the back of her upper thigh on his stomach. She then lifts and places the backs of her calves on his shoulder and leans back a little to place her palms on his thighs. She juts out her chest to give him a clear view of her breasts.

Pretzel

This pose is extremely aesthetically pleasing, and simply getting into this pose will make you two feel extremely sexy about each other. To perform the technique, both of you must sit face to face and kneel. You then close in, and the woman wraps her arms around the man. The woman lifts and places her left leg with the foot facing downwards next to the man's right foot, which must remain in its original pose, and his left leg is placed near her right foot, which must remain in its original pose. The man's hands can grab the woman's butt.

The Spread

The spread is a rudimentary but extremely sexy pose. It allows the woman great pleasure as she gets to caress her man and have him pleasure her. To perform the technique, the woman must sit on the edge of a sofa or table and spread her legs. The man stands in between her legs and enters her. She has his face close to her to kiss, and the man has his hands free.

The Intertwine

This pose can look impossible to mimic but can be extremely pleasurable if done correctly. The pose is extremely aesthetically pleasing. To perform this technique, both sit close to each other and face each other. The man must have his legs placed on either side of the woman. The woman then lifts both legs and places them on either side of his body below his underarms. His upper arms are supposed to lock her legs in place. The woman must then lift her upper arms and place them above his elbow. The man then lifts his legs and places them on top of the woman's hands. It might sound a bit tough, but the pose is guaranteed to reel in some good sex.

The G-Force

Easily the hottest tantric sex pose, the G-force is a piece de resistance. The man has control over the woman, but both parties derive amazing pleasure. To perform this technique, the woman must lie with her back on the bed, and the man must be by her legs and kneel. He then lifts her lower torso off the bed and balances her with her shoulder and head on the bed. Now he can either outstretch her legs to a 90-degree angle and enter or pull them down and place her feet just below his chest.

These are the various basic and sexy tantric sex positions that you can try with your partner to ignite a whole new level of passion.

Sofia Price

Conclusion

I hope this book provided you with the tools needed to help you fall in love with your partner all over again. I hope it was able to provide you with helpful tips that will help rekindle your relationship with your spouse or your significant other.

Falling in love is easy, and everything else that follows takes effort, consistency, patience, and unconditional love and support. Love and romance are sizzling during the initial stages of marriage. With time, we tend to grow more comfortable with each other and ourselves. This kind of comfort often leads to complacency. It is also perhaps one of the reasons why love starts fading away from marriages. However, the good news is that all this can be easily managed with a little effort. If you and your partner have committed to spending your life with each other, it's also important to ensure that the relationship stays healthy.

A marriage is like a plant. What will happen to a plant if it isn't regularly watered and doesn't get sufficient sunlight or nutrients? The plant will slowly wither away and die. The same thing happens to relationships when they aren't nurtured. As marriage is one of the most important relationships you will ever have in life, nurturing it is quite important. When it comes to marriage, a little effort certainly goes a long way.

In this book, you were introduced to different concepts that can rekindle love and romance in your relationship. Before you understand how to do all this, it's important to look at the different pillars of marriage and why love fades away. Learning to love yourself, nurturing the friendship, and reminiscing about the happy times are some simple techniques that can be used to strengthen the bond you share.

In this book, you also learned about improving your communication skills in marriage, understanding each other's love languages, and dealing with negative cycles. Apart from this, it included information about dealing with arguments, tips about advice and sympathy, using proactive therapy, and healing your marriage. Retaining the passion in a marriage is easy, but passion tends to go away with time. If you don't want this to happen to your marriage, it's important to rekindle the passion, ignite the sparks in the bedroom, and understand how to improve your sex life.

Your next step is to follow the tips, strategies, and techniques contained in this book. The information contained in this book will not help much unless they are applied. You can save your marriage and your relationship, and soon after applying the tips included in this book, you will notice that you are slowly falling in love with your partner once again.

Finally, if you enjoyed this book, then I'd like to ask you for a favor, would you be kind enough to leave a review for this book on Amazon? It'd be greatly appreciated!

Thank you, and good luck!

FREE E-BOOKS SENT WEEKLY

Join North Star Readers Book Club
And Get Exclusive Access To The Latest Kindle Books in Self-Improvement, Personal Health and Much More...

TO GET YOU STARTED HERE IS YOUR FREE E-BOOK:

www.northstarreaders.com/fearless-you

Sofia Price

References

https://www.thelawofattraction.com/love-yourself/

https://www.marcandangel.com/2015/05/10/16-simple-ways-to-love-yourself-again/

https://www.yourlaunchproject.com/launchblog/keep-happy-memories

https://firstthings.org/keys-to-effective-communication-in-marriage

https://www.psychalive.org/top-10-effective-communication-techniques-couples/

https://www.psychalive.org/communication-between-couples/

https://www.bolde.com/is-your-relationship-over-17-signs-the-love-is-gone/

https://www.aconsciousrethink.com/6343/falling-love-5-signs-feelings-fading/

https://www.researchgate.net/publication/233241159_Speaking_the_Language_of_Relational_Maintenance_A_Validity_Test_of_Chapman's_1992_Five_Love_Languages

https://globalnews.ca/news/3785280/7-ways-to-end-an-argument-with-your-partner/

https://www.oxfordtreatment.com/addiction-treatment/drug-therapy/couples/

https://www.marriage.com/advice/relationship/15-key-secrets-to-a-successful-marriage/

ARE YOU TRAPPED IN A VICIOUS CYCLE OF BROKEN RELATIONSHIPS?
DO YOU WANT TO BE ABLE TO FREE YOURSELF FROM THE NEGATIVITY THAT IS SEEMINGLY HOLDING YOU BACK??

This book will guide you through the process of defeating jealousy and gaining back your confidence and your life! Overcoming jealousy will help you nip insecurities in the bud and remove your reliance on material things and even other people for your own happiness. You can then begin to build loving and trusting relationships with the people important to you.

Here is what this book will teach you:

- Causes of your jealousy
- What jealousy says about you
- Dealing with jealousy from within
- Making meaningful connections
- Learning to love yourself
- Altering your view of reality
- Nurturing relationships
- Overcoming your fears

Visit to Order Your Copy Today!

www.amazon.com/dp/1514272326

WOULDN'T IT BE GREAT IF YOU COULD BE FREE FROM YOUR SHYNESS AND BE CONFIDENT ENOUGH TO STRIKE UP CONVERSATIONS?

Although many would say that you cannot let go of your true nature, everything is made possible if you set your mind to it. This book will teach you how to begin overcoming your shyness and realizing your true potential, both personally and professionally.

Here is what this book will help you learn:
- Determining the causes of your shyness
- Identifying the triggers that cause your anxiety
- Taking control of your own reactions
- Owning Your mind
- How to Build self-confidence
- How to improve relationships

Visit to Order Your Copy Today!

www.amazon.com/dp/1517495911

Made in United States
North Haven, CT
30 December 2021